Sarah,
Let's keep teaching
"how". xo God

Job Interview

Anxious? You've Got This!

Job Interview

Anxious? You've Got This!

Val Hunter

Job Interview
Anxious? You've Got This!

by Val Hunter

Mooncove Publishing

ISBN 978-0-9936-5810-5

The information provided herein is not a substitute for, nor meant to take the place of mental health care or treatment, or any prescribed therapies.

Unlike intermittent worries that can be expected to occur during a job search, clinically diagnosed anxiety, general anxiety disorders, panic disorders, social anxiety, PTSD, and adjustment disorders are long-term mental health conditions, with symptoms that can disrupt an individual's ability to engage in routine events and daily activities.

Anxiety disorders and other mental health challenges are best managed under the ongoing care of a physician and/or mental health practitioners and clinicians.

For the anxious job seeker

who gulps at the interview door,

and goes for it anyway.

Contents

Preface

WORK IS A CENTRAL ASPECT of life. It provides purpose and gives us meaning. That significance makes it difficult to separate our self-worth and identity from the day-to-day jobs we carry out.

So much so, that when asked, *what do you do?* it's easy to look past other ways in which we spend our time and talents, and respond about the job we perform day-to-day, as if our workaday tasks comprise the core of who we are and what we do.

As you move through these pages you'll be asked to acknowledge your attributes and strengths, and communicate the unique value that you will bring forward to your first, or next job.

> You can expect some anxiety to surface during your search for a job.

Whether you're a first-timer; a high school student or college grad; or you're employed but seeking career advancement;

Or, you're returning to work after a gap;

You might find yourself overwhelmed during a job search.

No one gets a free pass.

There are any number of challenges that are sure to pop up on your path.

That's why exploring your strengths and attributes is essential preparation prior to submitting job applications.

The time and effort you invest now to prepare will help you manage the bumps that wait somewhere on the road ahead.

Being prepared will also help soothe any anxious feelings that rise to the surface when you find yourself outside your comfort zone, where new challenges lie in wait for you.

One such challenge is the *job interview* – guaranteed to stand guard at the gateway to each and every job.

Then there's the dreaded question *Can you tell me about yourself?* that looms inside each and every job interview.

There's no escaping the job interview, and you must be ready to answer the *tell me about yourself* question. If you're not able to talk about yourself when you're asked, your distress at being caught unprepared can feel as if the ground has been pulled out from under your feet.

> *Imagine your panic when you can't find any words to tell the interviewer who you are. Without 'ground under your feet', it can feel as if you're standing at the open hatch of an airplane, several thousand feet in the air.*

Your imagination is potent.

A mere suggestion has placed you on the struts of an airplane!

> *Since you're standing there with the wind rushing against you, notice the weight of the parachute strapped to your back.*

Feel the pulse at your neck and your pounding heart in your throat, as the jump master shouts, 'Go!' and gives you a thumbs-up.

Will you take the leap and begin to prepare for the job interview process? It's your decision. In the past, feelings of anxiety may have held you back, or set limits on your experiences, under the pretext of keeping you safe.

Now you might consider using your feelings of uneasiness like a *tool* to measure your fears, and negotiate the actions you'll take, as you explore the challenges of a job interview.

The *more* you want *anything* – even a particular job – the greater your fear of loss, and the higher your level of anxiety.

It is often said that, similar to two sides of a coin, the <u>flip-side</u> of fear is excitement.

The future is always uncertain, and although excitement may be the furthest thing from your mind at this point in time, your awareness of both sides of anxiety provides balance and can even reduce your fears in the present moment.

When you take up the challenge, and start to practice the activities outlined in this book, everything you do to prepare will help you advance towards landing a job interview, with the mindfulness and communication skills to give it your best.

There's no need to lose the ground under your feet.

> You'll see progress when you intentionally take steps towards achieving your goals.

Start with doing *just one thing* differently – choose a *flip-side* behavior which is counter to the way you would typically approach a situation in which you feel stressed.

If, for example, you defer to others by habit when your friends or family discuss which movie the group wants to watch, or where to go for dinner, take a risk and voice your preference. The immediate change in how you and others perceive your new-found assertiveness is likely to astonish you.

> *You* are in charge of how you *feel*, prompted by the thoughts you *think*.

If you tend to withdraw or isolate when you're conflicted with something someone says or does, the next time you silently disagree with them, consider choosing behavior on the flip-side, and remain in their presence, despite your inner conflict.

Notice what happens when you stay in proximity with them, even though you don't say a word.

Later, in a minor conflict, you might feel the time is right for you to take a further risk, and let the other person know what you're feeling. *Even small steps forward can transform us.*

Our brains are built through what we *think, do*, and *feel*;

through *relationships* with the people who are in our lives;

and through our *experiences,* whether we are on our own, or with others.

Since the obstacles to achieving what we want are usually found in our daily routines, the decision you've made to step into the world of work, or to advance in your career is a perfect opportunity for you to begin to pattern your thoughts towards success for your future.

Here's how that works: the area of the brain that processes emotion develops before maturity occurs in the area of the brain that's responsible for cognition, thought, and judgment.

What is known as our *'emotional' brain* is the seat of habits and automatic behaviour, and is also the centre of our survival responses.

Anxiety is a survival response.

Lock this in: *our thoughts prompt our feelings.*

Expecting (thinking) the worst leads to feelings of anxiety.

Although habits and automatic actions occur below the level of our conscious thought, consistent mindful thought on our part is able to over-ride the reactions of the emotional brain, and set us on a new course.

The contents of our *thoughts* (both positive and negative) affect our *attitude* and *mood*, and how we spend our time.

Thinking in a *positive* way alters our *feelings* in a positive way. Positive *thinking* changes our *behaviour* in a positive way, too.

There's a saying that may help you remember the importance of your thinking patterns:

> *If I think the way I've always thought, I'll act the way I've always acted, and get what I've always got.*

This brings to mind one of my favourite sayings:

Change your thinking, change your life!

Try the mental prompt *think it*, *see it*, *say it*, and *do it* on for size, and see how it enlivens your imagination, develops your visualization skills, and urges you into action.

From this point forward, I invite you to begin to *think strong,* and intentionally choose behaviours that eventually will become habits that you've carefully chosen to support yourself to *grow strong*. With your attention on growing stronger, how about expanding your present routine around your *nutrition*, *sleep*, *movement*, and *exercise*? These four factors have enormous influence on mental health, resilience, and self-esteem.

While you're at it, now is a great time to start to bring in situations and experiences that excite your thoughts and inspire you to hope.

Stay strong here. This sounds complicated, but you *can* take this on. *Even small steps matter.* Just start somewhere. Anywhere.

Almost *everyone* can benefit from a tune-up to their daily routine.

For balance, utilize any of the positive change you've set in motion and start a mini practice of meditation and mindfulness as a way to soothe your thoughts. *Or simply relax, stretch your limbs, and breathe!*

Progressive habits, either those mentioned here, or other techniques you already practice, will build active pathways in the brain to help you accomplish your goals. Do what you can to get started. The rest will fall into place.

Jot notes in the margins of this book. And use a journal or notebook as a daily companion.

> ## Writing about your insights provides context and form as you blend in new information.
>
> ## Write, and watch your strength matrix grow!

As you move along the path to the job you want, you'll discover that *preparation is magic!*

Preparation eases tension and stress, removes fear, and calms an anxious mind.

Preparing for what you want will set you up to practice, practice again, and when you're sure that you've got everything down pat, the foundation you've built will encourage you to practice even more.

Preparation feeds your self-confidence. And preparation remains with you when times are hard, and things get tough.

Preparation is the habit you'll depend on as you advance through these pages. It's the accountability that will keep you on track.

Preparation will battle with your doubts, balance your thoughts, and regardless of the outcome, all of your practice and prep will help you remain strong throughout the job interview process.

Once again, take a moment to activate your imagination.

Notice that you and I are standing together on the struts of the airplane!

Are you ready to take that leap with me?

Dear Job Seeker,

Competing for a job is not for the faint of heart. The need to earn money, your concerns about the future, and the uncertainty that casts a shadow throughout the job search process are bound to make you feel anxious.

Inside this book you'll find creative ideas, concrete strategies, and practical tools that have helped countless others, including myself, during our own bouts of job search anxiety, jitters, and nerves. These mindfulness tools have supported us to thrive on our own paths to employment, and beyond.

Mindful techniques that help you adjust the way you usually approach challenges, build self-acceptance, and remain in the moment won't completely erase your job search nervousness and interview anxiety. But these efforts can provide you with some temporary relief from distress.

Trust yourself to explore and experiment. Take from here anything that fits for you, and leave the rest behind.

You won't be fearless when you approach the interview door, but when you've incorporated the techniques that work for you, and you face that door, your fear will have lost the intensity of its grip.

On the flip-side of your anxiety, you'll be more able to step forward, *despite the fear*.

First jobs are important first steps. You might ask, *What would be the best first job for me?* to which my answer is, *Your best first job is your first job! Start preparing. Get ready to be interviewed, and get yourself hired. Embrace your first job, give it your best, and watch yourself rise.*

If you're presently under-employed, if you've decided to return to work after some time away, or you're establishing yourself in the gig economy, there'll be moments you'll feel out of touch, and unsure of your value. You might wonder if you ever had, or still have what it takes. Let's work together to restore your confidence. *Your best job is your next job! Start preparing. Get ready to be interviewed, and get yourself hired. Embrace your next job, give it your best, and watch yourself rise.*

Fully commit to this process, and the job you've been seeking will find you. It's waiting for you to claim it, on the other side of the interview door.

You've got this!

Val

Chapter 1

YOUR JOURNEY

Prepare, practice, and repeat.
Trust the process.

Curiosity and Mindfulness

CURIOSITY IS THE MAP YOU'LL WANT ON BOARD for the journey you're about to take. When you remain curious about your process, countless possibilities will become apparent, and each and every step you take forward will help build awareness of your strengths and abilities.

Mindfulness acts like a compass that will help you stay on track. And when you're outside your comfort zone, being mindful will help to soothe your nerves.

The Plan

You'll be called to take steps that are on the *flip-side* of your usual way of doing things, or on the *other side of the coin* of your behaviour. Proceed cautiously. Take mindful risks after you've considered both sides of things, and you feel safe.

Though the steps you take will be incremental and relatively small, sometimes the ground under your feet might become challenging and difficult. But one degree at a time, the terrain will eventually even out, and progress will be do-able.

Two foundational skills will highlight the groundwork of your job-seeking journey:
- *choice*

and the liberating notion of
- *personal accountability.*

When you embrace the concept of *choice*, your awareness of your responsibility for *how you see yourself* and therefore *how others perceive you* is clear. Out of that awareness you can begin to redefine your self-concept, and perhaps decide to reactivate any elements of yourself that have been set aside.

You're invited to try on progressive new behaviours that will have a positive impact on you, and ultimately the way others see you.

Repetition and practice will help you incorporate these new communication skills and behaviours.

The changes you make will have an impact on your personal growth – a powerful reason to trust yourself, experiment, and celebrate positive choices that cultivate new sides of yourself.

The tool of *personal accountability* helps us explore situations in which we find ourselves.

Through examining the choices we've made, accountability allows us to consider our part in various situations in which we play a central role.

And accountability helps us replace any previous self-judgments with compassion for ourselves.

As you make strong new choices, your accountability will shine a spotlight on your success, and reveal how, through your flip-side actions, *you* have set up all of your accomplishments.

If you want a result you've never had, take a risk: do something you've never done.

Personal accountability is never about blame. Assuming accountability for the *choices* you've made reflects your awareness and self-responsibility.

Even if you're unable to embrace the notion of personal accountability, or can't make the connection between being accountable and having set up the events that have occurred, it's useful to assume accountability for the way in which you *respond* to the *events* in your life.

Process and Outcome

Imagine that you parachuted out of the plane and have landed at the edge of a vibrant forest. You're ready to ditch your parachute and venture forth.

You feel the warmth of the sun on your shoulders. You hear crows caw and chipmunks chatter. A leaf falls onto the cover of a book that lies at your feet. You glance at the title – 'Job Interview – Anxious? You've Got This!'

You reach for the book, and tuck it under your arm.

A path leads into the woods.

A sign says, 'This way'.

Your heart pounds! Everything is new. You feel excited and nervous at the same time.

The journey you take through the woods is your process. Sometimes your process will be referred to as your *path* or *experience*.

In this book you'll encounter many ideas and suggestions.

But the only *rule* on this learning journey is *be kind to yourself*.

No one is perfect. Everyone has flaws. Imperfections are surface blemishes, and not a reflection of your true self.

Here, and on other journeys you'll take in your life, the compassion you have for yourself and your actions will encourage you to keep exploring, and reaching forward.

Every process requires some action on our part – although we're not always aware of being in a particular process, or that we're responsible for the actions we take. For example, although we might be able to acknowledge being anxious about meeting new people, we might be unaware that we're frequently unavailable for social get-togethers. Every outcome is the result of events, both the events that have been set up deliberately and those that are unintentional, and have occurred during a process.

The need to have a wish come true can start the process of pursuing a goal.

But beyond any starting point, mere wishing has no power.

By itself, *wishing* you'll land a specific job, or any job at all, won't result in the outcome for which you've wished.

If you're set on being hired, *wishing to be hired* must transform in your thinking into *wanting to be hired.*

Wanting to be hired must evolve into *willing to do whatever it takes.*

When your *wish* matures through each of these steps, the eventual result could be *having a job.*

To simplify, the steps in the process of accomplishing what you want are *wishing, wanting, willing, having.*

Goal-setting helps us stay on track, develop, grow, remain hopeful, and go after what we want.

But if we do something *mainly* for a particular outcome, goal, or result, rather than the process itself – it's easy to lose sight of the journey we're on.

Life happens on the journey.

Stay curious. Intentionally curious. *Make curiosity your super power.* Ask questions. Seek answers.

When you pay attention to your thoughts– in other words – when you strive to understand the moment, you can use your curiosity to lead you.

You might notice that being preoccupied with the future pulls you out of the present moment; into feeling worried and vulnerable, and maybe even into judging yourself and your actions.

Being fearful and self-judging is often a sign that we're no longer curious about what's happening in the present.

Concentrating on the final step in a process – instead of the process itself, keeps your mind in the *past* where you can get stuck on previous losses, self- judgment, and regret; in the *future* where you can get caught up in worry and anxiety; or *inside an exhausting cycle* in which your thoughts ruminate over the events of the past, and possibilities, or dire events that may occur in the future. The past is past. The future isn't here yet.

When you catch yourself fretting over the past or worrying about the future, text yourself a reminder to pick up the worry later, at a specific appointed time.

Tell your brain, *Stop processing!* Then, even if you can only manage to stop over-thinking for a moment at a time, intentionally bring yourself back into the present, and celebrate your triumph. Tell yourself, *I've got this!*

At the appointed time you've set up to continue worrying, follow through on your commitment – re-look the issue, and decide if you want to ruminate. If you choose to move on, text yourself a reminder to pick up the issue again, at a later time.

> To stay on track, nudge yourself back into your process when you notice brooding thoughts or self-judgments start to edge their way in.

Preparing for a job interview is a complex process, made up of many different life tasks, objectives, challenges, and skills. All of these aspects of the interview process provide opportunities for growth and change, regardless of the final outcome.

We have countless ways to manage our process. For example, some of us are highly spontaneous, make free-form decisions, and appear comfortable making choices *in the moment*.

Decision-makers fall along a range, all the way from spur-of-the-moment deciders, to others of us at the far end of the scale who tend to *focus on the future*, and appear more comfortable goal-setting and charting our progress in a predictable step-by-step manner.

Challenge yourself to experiment, and try decision-making strategies at the opposite end of your comfort range. Free-form, conservative strategies, and numerous other approaches along the span are valid, and you'll see from your experimentation that each is enhanced when balanced with other styles.

At this point, start to create a plan, with manageable steps, for the type of job you'd like to pursue. You are at the beginning of a new outlook. Eventually, as your plan develops, you should be able to identify anxious thought patterns that may have restricted your progress in the past.

As with everything in life, you don't have to figure it all out at once.

Preparation, Practice, and Rehearsal

Change starts with your thoughts. Your thoughts can provide new choices.

Mindfulness can help you think your way out of an attack of nerves.

At the same time, the part of your brain that processes emotion will be encouraged by your mindfulness to lay down fresh tracks in an attempt to over-ride the fear-based ones.

Most of us have at least one limiting fear.

Some of us are afraid to climb a ladder, some are terrified to speak in groups, while others feel awkward eating alone in public places, because these actions are outside our particular comfort zones.

> Your comfort zone, similar to a fence or boundary, has been placed around various feelings and behaviours, to make you feel safe.

Through long-term conditioning and a great deal of practice inside each of your comfort zones, much of what you *do*, a lot of what you *say*, and even *the way in which you say it* has become automatic, based on habits you established to protect the varied aspects of your life.

Gradually, by following the same patterns or habits, your comfort zones have made it easy for you to manage day-to-day activities. Ordinary details such as the clothes you wear, your daily routines, the things you value, the friends you choose, how you spend your down-time, and the outcomes you strive for, all fit inside a variety of comfort zones.

> Over time, our habitual behavior becomes automatic.

When children experience hurtful criticism and disapproval, they might learn to shut down, perhaps having decided to withhold their thoughts and ideas to keep themselves safe from unwarranted criticism.

In another strategy, although a person might be comfortable *responding* to questions, in order to protect themselves from criticism, their particular comfort zone may keep them from *volunteering* that same information.

Our individual comfort zones are carefully organized and structured, and they contain most of what we need psychologically, so we're able to function 'safely' in the world with others.

Inside each comfort zone everything has a place, and as long as the comfort zone is able to function without being challenged, nothing changes.

For routine activities, this can be useful.

However, if our anxiety is conditioned into daily habit so that our psychological need for safety and protection over-rides our ability to choose to experience life outside our comfort zone, our anxiety can manifest into any number of physical symptoms and conditions.

Anxious thoughts about a past event or future situation can feel unmanageable.

Anxiety and nerves can make us feel unwell, and often manifest as digestive upsets and sleep issues.

You might have experienced being awakened in the night in an episode of over-thinking, and found it difficult to fall back to sleep.

Sleep deprivation can set off a cascade of irritability, headaches, and difficulty focusing.

Chronic fatigue amplifies our agitation and forgetfulness. Some people become fragile and tearful. Some avoid contact out of fear they'll start crying and won't be able to stop.

At the extreme, these and other psychological needs and physical symptoms restrict our experiences, leading to isolation, limiting freedom and interaction.

Each of our various comfort zones are programmed by previous experiences, in a similar way that a thermostat, once it is set, kicks in when the temperature of a room is out of range.

Resetting the thermostat in your living room is a relatively quick and easy event that calls for minimal skills, but stretching the boundaries of a comfort zone is an intentional process that requires learning new skills through *preparation*, *practice*, and *rehearsal*.

At the core of the experience of stretching the boundaries of your comfort zone is your desire to expand the limits that have restrained you.

Then you can engage your strengths in new directions that might be exciting, but may be somewhat terrifying, too.

The terror can be dealt with. Preparation, if you recall, is magic.

When you take in new information, and practice and repeat effective new skills, the inner strengthening adds to your confidence and ability.

There is no wasted energy!

Everything you do builds on your experience.

If you haven't already engaged an ally or support buddy in your process, now is the time to do it. Allies and support buddies should be unconditional in their support, without offering advice. They should listen, sometimes question your responses for clarity, and reflect back what they hear you say.

Choose the best person for the job – someone who cares about you, and will nudge you in order to support you in your process, but will not interfere with your choices. These traits in an ally are not negotiable.

Don't let age be a factor, just find your ally. Here's a hint: we sometimes overlook the supportive, willing, and eagerly available very young and very old.

Chapter 2

YOUR TOOLS

Aim for progress. Not perfection.

Imagination: A Mighty Device!

IMAGINE *on the ground in front of you is a balance beam, twelve inches wide, twelve inches thick, and fifty feet in length.*

In your mind's eye, see yourself step up onto the balance beam. Observe yourself standing on the beam.

Turn on the beam and face in the opposite direction.

Pivot again and face the full length of the beam.

Take a few steps forward. Stop. Bend your knees in a deep squat and straighten up.

Bounce a little. Notice how the beam feels under your feet.

Be aware of what it feels like to stand on the beam, twelve inches off the ground.

Close your eyes.

Take one step forward. Feel the beam under your feet.

Take another step forward.

Inch yourself along. You're doing great.

Now stand still on the beam with your eyes closed. Notice your breathing.

Open your eyes. Take five steps forward and stop.

You've mastered the balance beam. Feel your heart swell with pride.

Still balancing on the beam, feel the beam gently lift and rise fifty feet above the ground.

Take a step forward.

What just happened?

Your brain can't tell if an event is real or imagined!

From here on, I encourage you to use your imagination intentionally and sensibly, and to exercise it often. For example, to learn to deal with an aspect of your anxiety, *think of something that you fear doing or saying*. In your mind's eye, *see or hear yourself doing or saying that thing you fear*.

Congratulate yourself for doing in your imagination what you're afraid of doing in real life, and then challenge yourself to *practice doing it in real life* anyway, despite your fear.

The implications for the use of imagination as you stretch yourself and the boundaries of your comfort zone are encouraging. You don't have to be an elite athlete, or other high-performance human. You just need to *set your focus*, *commit to your practice,* and *do it*. What is it that you want to accomplish? *How about a job interview in which you demonstrate strong interpersonal skills while you present the very best version of yourself?*

Imagine that you can, and you've already accomplished it, in your mind.

Soon you'll be ready, and prepared to go after the job you want, and claim it!

Attention

Attention is your focused awareness of the present moment.

Anxiety and worry, which are symptoms of mind-chatter, disrupt our ability to pay attention and be in the moment.

Focused attention helps build resilience, and gives us a conscious say in how we choose to spend the moment.

An interview is one such moment. The level of your focused attention in the interview depends on your ability to concentrate on the interviewer and the situation. Don't let your nervousness distract you, and trick you into putting your attention on something or someone other than the person interviewing you. Strange as it might sound, we become distracted as a way to soothe our jitters.

Beware is actually *be aware*. Don't let yourself get caught by the distraction troll!

> ## Focused attention helps you remain present when you're in stressful situations.

Focused attention is a critical skill to have when you're interviewing for a job, and for your life beyond the interview. Practice, preparation, and rehearsal will help you develop your focus.

Focus your attention so you can manage your anxiety. Then plan to have a successful interview!

Your attention to your interviewer's presence – the words they speak, and their actions – will show them that you have respect for, and interest in them and what they are saying.

Intention

Your *intention* is your conscious awareness of a goal, target, or an outcome that you desire and which you're determined to accomplish.

Having an intention means that you're present, and have mindfully chosen to focus at that particular moment in time on what you want to actualize, then, or in the future.

After you've formulated an intention in your mind, your intention, similar to any other goal, creates a *pattern* and *format* when you write it down.

When you formulate your intention, you should be *specific* and *concrete*.

- Your intention should be stated as if it's already actualized in the *present tense*. For example:

  I am speaking with confidence in my interview with Starbucks. Be sure to be exact so there is no mistake in your unconscious mind about what it is you say you want.

- Your intention should be *measureable*:

  indicate how much, when, and where. For example, *I am being interviewed at my ideal location, in Kitsilano.*

- You should also *predict the feeling* that your intention will bring:

  state the feeling as if it has already happened. For example, *I am relaxed, confident, and joyful.*

Set your intention and observe what happens.

Use your thinking to balance feelings of anxiety with thoughts about your ability.

To stay on track, read your intention statements several times a day, every day.

There's no limit to the number of intentions you can have.

> Smile broadly as you read or repeat your intention statements.
>
> And as with all of your declarations, be sure to say them aloud.

Choice (Risk and Trust)

Each morning, a useful way to organize your brain for the day ahead is to set your intention, which has a direct bearing on your *risk readiness*.

Risk readiness is your willingness to *take a hopeful leap,* face your fear, and venture away from the old familiar anxiety that waits, ready to pounce, from the edge of your comfort zone.

You *can* hack your brain. The trick is to thwart the anxiety troll, and engage fully in some degree of risk, even for a very short time.

A brief moment, just a mere second, can stall that anxiety goblin.

It is often said that 99% effort is really difficult. As you've probably experienced, *the smallest amount of resistance* or doubt can take control of your mood, and ruin your entire day.

100% effort is easy because there's no resistance once you've committed, and put yourself all in.

Engage fully. *This is about training your brain.*

Try on a new behavior for one minute at a time.

Then do the un-do-able.

The power is in your hands. You're the only person able to direct the change you want to see in yourself.

Do the un-do-able for a brief *one minute at a time*.

If you struggle with anxiety around people you don't know, typical flip-side actions are to ask a question of a safe stranger: perhaps place an order with a cashier in a fast food restaurant, or ask directions from a transit driver. When you take on unfamiliar actions, after you've done so, pause and celebrate, because you *did* it! When you feel you're ready, up the ante, and extend your risk readiness in the next action you undertake by one minute more, and so on.

If we're fearful of venturing into crowded places alone, but we're learning to build our risk readiness, for the first time ever we might stand at the ticket window of a movie theatre, enter the lobby, choose our preferred seat, and silently cheer our accomplishment. Taking small but bold steps, we've risked attending a movie alone! Simple, progressive steps move us forward. *The key is to ensure that our small bold steps are genuinely flip-side actions that stretch us.*

Then assess yourself on a continuum from your usual level of anxiety all the way to comfort and competency. With each progressive step you take, observe how you feel.

To get a sense of what competency feels like – trust yourself, and set your anxiety aside for the moment.

Anxious feelings serve a purpose for all of us. We'll never entirely give up our relationship with anxiety.

Every time you choose to take a measured risk, your fear is diminished for the moment. In that moment, you'll engage in the particular activity with increased confidence.

This step can lead you towards a new way of being, and lay the groundwork for developing a new competency.

For many of us, our new-found confidence stirs renewed interest in our health and well-being, which includes getting in touch with our body's strength and abilities.

Claiming competency in your life begins with your physical self.

Our bodies are miraculous instruments that we often fail to acknowledge.

When our thoughts are in the present, we begin to sync with our body's natural rhythms. To get there, it won't be necessary to push yourself. Just respect what your body needs.

Anxious thoughts wreak havoc on sleep patterns and cause us to distrust our bodies, and by extension, ourselves.

Sleeping and waking times are the book-ends to our days.

Without regulated sleep, we can become isolated from others.

We begin to learn to trust ourselves when we follow through and do the things we know we can do, with no excuses.

A daily action you can take to reinforce trust in yourself is to go to bed, to sleep, at a routine time every night.

If you decide 10 pm is a suitable bedtime, put yourself to bed at 10 pm every night. Soon you'll notice that your waking time settles into a predictable daily pattern. When you wake up, get up. Use your notebook to record your bedtime and waking times, and any thoughts that you're inspired to write concerning this phenomenon.

There are no small steps. Every step you take forward is progress.

Choose to do the next thing you know you can, and step by step, your self-trust will grow.

Strength Contract

You might be aware that you have some degree of negative self-talk that affects how you *feel*, although maybe you're unaware of how much your thoughts – both positive and negative – affect your *behaviour*.

> Brain science tells us our brains change daily, based on what we *do*, what we *say*, what we *think*, and what we *feel*.

The *thoughts* you think and the *words* you speak have a significant impact on your *feelings* and *actions*.

You can learn to harness the force of your words through the use of strength-based personal statements that are known as *affirmations*. A simple example of a strength-based statement or affirmation is *My thoughts and words are packed with power.*

Repeating affirmations helps manage and even over-ride your fears, nervousness, limiting beliefs, and negative self-talk – while they go to work to re-set your thinking.

> At the very least, affirmations are tools you can use to soothe your anxiety.

Affirmations are effective whether you silently read them, or say them out loud, and they provide additional reassurance if you memorize and call them to mind throughout the day.

As you affirm your strengths several times daily, and you personalize your statements using the words *my* and *I* you'll notice that your thinking shifts towards a more positive self-view, which begins to neutralize negative self-talk and any thoughts that limit you.

An effective tool for grounding yourself in your personal strength is to *intentionally* focus on a statement that affirms a quality or action that has challenged you in the past.

This type of affirmation is known as a *strength contract* – a contract that you make with yourself which validates your ability to overcome challenges, stated as if you've already conquered whatever challenges might be on your path at the moment.

Strength contracts always start with the words, '*I AM*'. Even just the words '*I AM*' stated on their own, form a powerful affirmation, while keeping your attention in the moment!

When you tag onto 'I AM', a word or phrase that empowers and affirms you, this very brief and validating statement helps you claim the part of you that embodies a source of your strength, while it grounds you in self-confidence.

Compose a personalized strength contract that you feel affirms you. There are infinite possibilities. Below are some examples to get you started:

I AM   trusting myself and others.

I AM   going with the flow.

I AM   well-spoken.

I AM   able, learning, and growing.

I AM   making good decisions.

I AM   prepared to move forward.

I AM   calm and collected.

I AM   powerful and capable.

I AM   worth it here and now.

I AM   taking good care of me.

I AM   enthusiastic.

I AM   strong and smart.

I AM   a gift.

I AM   making a difference.

I AM   clear and definite.

I AM   voicing my value.

I AM   committed to good things.

I AM   loveable.

I AM   a force for good.

I AM   in control of my destiny.

I AM   ready and able to work.

I AM   thoughtful and kind.

I AM   resilient.

I AM   worthy of being heard.

I AM   in touch with my potential.

I AM   following my heart.

I AM   hardworking and competent.

I AM   taking charge of my life.

I AM   letting go.

I AM   balancing my needs with the needs of others.

I AM giving my best effort.

I AM asking for feedback and learning from it.

Jot down several strength contracts here, and try them on for size. You'll know when you've hit on the perfect statement!

I AM ...

I AM ...

I AM ...

Smile and repeat your contract over and over.

Say your strength contract silently. *Say it out loud.* Sing it. *See yourself being your contract!*

In the beginning, you might have to *imagine* you are what you say you are, in order for you to believe the truth about yourself.

Eventually you'll *know* that you are *what* and *who* you say you are!

Try some more strength contracts on for size. Jot them down, smile, and repeat each of them again and again.

I AM ...

I AM ...

As you think and speak these positive statements you're building healthy thought pathways in your brain.

You're becoming self-reliant, stronger, and more capable every moment.

Something to remember: you can never repeat your contract too much!

And now here's a strength-building *getting to know and appreciate yourself* exercise that I encourage you to practice often, after you're ready for the day:

> *Stand in front of a well-lit mirror. Look into your eyes, and smile.*
>
> *Hold your smile, and gaze into your eyes for 30 seconds. Notice the galaxy that exists in each of your eyes.*

Count the seconds silently.

Take a few moments to write about the experience.

Communication

As you sit silently in a coffee shop scrolling through your phone, not intentionally communicating with anyone, you're actually passing on information about yourself through your clothing, the way you style your hair, your posture, breathing, movements, gaze behaviour, where you're sitting, your relationship with others, the objects in your possession, and so much more!

There's power in knowing that everything you do, in fact, all of your behaviour *means something.* In other words, all of your actions and behaviour communicate information about you. To state it another way, every behaviour has communication value, and since your actions speak for you, you can use this knowledge to your best advantage.

In studies of nonverbal communication, which is commonly referred to as body language, it was found that when a communication message was conveyed, a mere 7% of the message came from the actual words that were spoken.

It was found that vocal elements like tone of voice, rate of speech, volume, and inflection made up about 38% of the message that was conveyed; but a whopping 55% of the message was transmitted through body movements, posture, facial expressions, and gestures.

When you add up the aspects of vocal elements and body language, the total nonverbal message impact is a staggering 93%!

The takeaway from this is enlightening. The way in which you deliver your message nonverbally is more important than the words you choose!

You cannot not communicate!

The word *'communication'* derives from Latin words that mean *'to make common'* and *'to share'*.

In addition to the powerful nonverbal messages that are relayed, your spoken words are also laden with symbolic information.

When you meet someone for the first time, both you and they immediately and automatically start to search for common ground. The questions and answers each of you share reveal how much you and they are focused on the interaction. Your responses also indicate the level of curiosity each of you has about the other. Mutual curiosity will help both of you feel accepted, and more likely to continue your conversation.

If you're anxious during a conversation or interaction but want it to continue, being curious about the other person is an effective way for you to take your mind off your own discomfort, which will help you remain in the moment.

When we communicate with others we look for cues or some signs that they want to connect with us.

Your efforts to engage with curiosity during a job interview will have a bearing on your personal experience of the interview, as well as the outcome.

Since a key to establishing and maintaining a connection is to consciously stay attentive and curious, one way to enhance your curiosity is to become more aware of the people around you. When you're nervous or anxious – *especially when you're nervous or anxious* – make a point of *talking to the eyes*.

When you're around friends and family, practice looking into their eyes for a moment when they're close by. Look just long enough for you to identify the colour of their eyes. Don't worry; if they notice – just smile and compliment their eyes.

Think to yourself, *I'm looking at brown eyes,* or, *I'm looking at green eyes*, or whatever colour eyes you see.

That's it. Do it over and over, with people you know.

In the brief moment it takes to *talk to the eyes* you'll raise your connectivity with others and expand your comfort zone.

Since you know that we communicate to ourselves through our *thoughts*, and the *words* we choose to speak, and you're aware that the *quality* of our *self-talk* affects our *feelings* and *behavior*, below are some reinforcing words and phrases to jot in your notebook, read aloud, and practice.

Yes!

I can.

I will.

I'll give it my best shot.

I'm good at that.

Thanks!

That's really interesting!

I like that.

I'm excited!

Will you help me?

Here you go.

I'm glad to give you a hand with that.

I feel great!

Challenge yourself *daily* to fit these words and phrases into your conversations with others.

Go for it!

Notice when positively framed words and phrases alter your experience and change the way you feel and act.

Although there's no one who knows you better than you know yourself, being asked to talk about yourself can push a panic button.

Imagine you're in a social setting and someone extends their hand in greeting. They want to know more about you, and they say some variation of *Can you tell me about yourself?* which is so often used as an ice-breaker to start conversations, the question has become iconic.

In fact, you'll be asked this question countless times in your own life. If you feel put on the spot and haven't thought about or practiced an answer to the question your likely response will be, *I'm not good at talking about myself.* Meanwhile, the clock is ticking and you'll be at a loss as you struggle to find something to say.

Whenever our anxiety takes over, things get awkward fast.

Whether you're in social situations, or at a job interview, the first impressions that people have of you (and that you have of them) are difficult to erase from memory. First impressions really do matter.

I encourage you to *prepare and memorize at least two best-case answers to the question Can you tell me about yourself?* A *formal response* will be essential for job search, work, and similar situations; and a *casual answer* that you're able to deliver in a comfortable, natural way will come in handy in countless *social situations*.

Answering the question *Can you tell me about yourself?* is an expectation you'll have to meet in *every* job interview!

Therefore, creating a response to the question *Can you tell me about yourself?* which you'll adjust to fit the job for which you're applying, is *the most important task* you can undertake now, as you prepare for future job interviews.

If the only thing you do from here forward is prepare your own authentic answer to *Can you tell me about yourself?* you'll be miles ahead of the competition for any job.

But there's so much more for you to gain from this process!

The strategies outlined in these pages will help you manage your anxiety, so you can succeed over the long run when stressful events happen, long after you've landed your job. This race you're running covers a long distance.

Too many people overlook the value of preparation. Unaware they've signed up for a marathon, they make a fast dash to what they think is the end point. But sadly, for them, the place at which they stop isn't the actual finish line.

Instead of making a fast dash, pace yourself.

After you've taken time to prepare a *tell me about yourself* response, when someone asks you – instead of panicking – you can enjoy your new-found confidence, easily answer their question, and reflect the best of yourself. *That's the finish line!*

Okay, big breath.

Do you celebrate yourself through your words?

What's the story you tend to tell about yourself most often? Is your story about yourself all positive? Is it all negative?

Learning to balance both sides of the story that you tell yourself and others about the person you are is an important habit to cultivate. The image you hold of yourself matters. Think of yourself as *able*. Reflect on your attributes and achievements.

If you're not yet comfortable with writing down the concrete results you've achieved to this point in your life, start by listing the qualities you possess that make you a good human, such as empathy, kindness, thoughtfulness, sharing, and respect for others – and go from there.

Communicate positive self-statements. *From this point forward*, only think and speak about yourself with respect for yourself as a worthy human being, and talk about your accomplishments with pride.

Use your imagination as a mechanism for your greater good. Practice *smile-talking* about yourself in the privacy of your own room, and very soon you'll be more poised and self-confident when you tell others who you are.

You are who you *think you are*, and who you *say you are!*

Chapter 3

YOUR FEARS

Predict the best outcome possible.

The Fear Response

WHEN A THREATENING EVENT OCCURS, the effects of fear are felt in the body, even when the physical body isn't threatened.

The *emotional brain*, which is the headquarters for survival instincts that are activated in the fear response, evolved when you were an infant, long before you had the ability to think things through.

That's why the feeling state of anxiety is so deeply rooted, and is resistant to thoughts. At every stage of life, a threat to your physical or emotional safety will trigger the fear response in a flash.

The *fear* that is familiar to all of us is a survival mechanism that is activated with urgency by any perceived danger, in the part of the brain called the *amygdala* – a set of neurons that are responsible for processing our emotions.

When you perceive danger and become fearful, or when you experience a threat to your mental, emotional, or physical self, your amygdala signals the adrenal glands to begin to release into your blood stream the stress hormones, adrenaline and noradrenaline. This activates the automatic stress response of *fight, flight,* or *freeze,* to prepare you to fight or flee the danger.

At this point, your heart rate speeds up and your blood pressure rises. Blood pounds in your head, while your breathing becomes rapid and shallow, and your eyes dart. These primitive reactions are meant to prepare you to encounter an assailant. Blood that rushes to your extremities allows you to stand and fight the perceived danger, or run from it. Accordingly, your hands tighten and forearms become heavy, and you become hyper-alert, anxious, and ready to defend, despite the fact that an assailant is not ever likely to appear!

All of these primitive reactions are automatic, generated from the emotional aspect of your brain. They don't require any conscious decisions on your part.

In primitive times, you might have faced a saber-tooth tiger and perhaps clubbed it over the head, or maybe you ran from it as fast as you could. In either case, if you caught sight of a second tiger stalking you, it's likely you would have frozen in fear right there on the spot.

Today, it's uncommon to have to defend ourselves physically. More probable at this point in time, the threat we perceive would be directed towards our thoughts and feelings.

No matter the threat, the stress responses of fight, flight, and freeze are hard-wired into our brains.

Earlier, when you used your imagination to explore the balance beam, your brain believed the experience, because it's unable to distinguish between a real event and an imagined one.

A threat is a threat, despite whether the danger is mental, emotional, physical, or imagined. The stress responses that we feel are in reaction to our fear of a *perceived* attack, whether or not actual danger exists. Regardless, the same primitive responses occur.

Your stress response is activated and you prepare to *fight* or *flee*.

Sometimes, as with the second tiger stalking you, the terror is so great you cannot move.

> When you're terrified, your *cognition* – the *thinking part of you* – freezes.

That's why it's difficult to form a coherent sentence when you're angry, or why you struggle to remember a fact or detail when you're rattled.

Later, when the threat passes, your fear subsides, and you get your brain back.

The Anxiety Response

If you feel anxious, you're not alone.

Anxiety, which is *closely connected to fear*, is another automatic stress response during which your amygdala, when triggered by external events, sends signals to the adrenal glands to release stress hormones into your blood stream.

Uncertainty about the future is a reality for many of us, and uncertainty and worry can quickly set the anxiety response into motion.

Although some people may seem invincible, anxiety can be provoked in any of us.

When we're anxious, our brain is focused on the future, and *predicts that something bad is about to happen.* This puts us out of balance.

At any life stage, and especially during stressful times such as a job search, anxiety can strike when our thoughts about *accepting* that we don't know what the future holds, and *wondering* what lies ahead of us tip out of balance. Our thoughts might begin to morph into *worrying* about the future.

When we're out of balance we talk too much, tell too much, ask too much, control too much — and sometimes do the opposite of any of those actions.

Even when we're just a little bit nervous, our sense organs are on high alert. When that happens, we easily fall back on our automatic behavior, and retreat into a comfort zone where our choices are limited to a restricted range of options. As an example, for some of us, the fear of punishment in childhood resulted in hyper-obedient adolescents and adults who, despite being grown, are terrified of judgment.

Paradoxically, if at some point we become anxious and retreat to the emotional safety of a comfort zone, our anxious response may be perceived by others as an indication that we're oppositional. Sadly, anxious youth are too often labelled difficult and oppositional, when their behavior is anything but.

The stress responses of *anxiety* tend to be *flight* and *freeze*.

> Once the anxiety response is set in motion, the effects can be long-term and enduring.

As with the fear response, the activation of anxiety causes the brain to repeatedly signal the release of stress hormones until the mind eventually quiets, as a result of whatever conscious or unconscious methods are used to soothe the distress.

Whether you experience *fear* or *anxiety*, your brain registers that you're in danger.

> Fear is a quick dash, while anxiety can feel more like a long-distance foot race, that's run barefoot over jagged glass.

It bears repeating: it doesn't matter if the danger is *real* or if it's *imagined*.

You may feel uncomfortable in conflict situations. If your automatic stress response is to *flee* disagreements, you'll leave. In the extreme, maybe you won't show up at all.

If you're afraid of appearing foolish, you might withhold your ideas and thoughts, perhaps choke up when you disagree with someone, or become tearful in the face of criticism.

When your thoughts are overwhelmed by the stress of the situation, you're likely to *freeze*; and be unable to gather your thoughts.

Just as in the fear response, when we feel anxious and stressed, our cognition shuts down. You might remember being called on in school to give an answer you were unsure of, and under the pressure to respond, your brain suddenly went blank. That's what happens when cognition shuts down. *When we're anxious, the functions of thinking, remembering, and sorting simple details become a colossal struggle.*

Fear and anxiety are brain events, triggered by our thoughts.

Mindfulness restores cognition and over-rides anxious thoughts by placing our awareness in the present moment — which is the only point at which we are free from worry. This mindfulness process doesn't happen by chance. It's intentional, and requires some effort and directed attention.

Fear, Anxiety and the Brain: A Mindful Approach

Over time, fear and anxiety, activated by thoughts that are often below the level of consciousness can become an automatic defense against attempting new behaviours, participating in new experiences, and venturing into a new physical or psychological territory.

Moving forward and unwinding our automatic responses requires us to bring mindfulness into the process, with the awareness that long-standing anxious thought patterns can readily slip forward and take control of our thinking.

> Anxious thoughts can be a useful nudge to remind you to focus on your breathing, and take steps to return your thoughts into balance.

Calming our anxiety through the mindful state of relaxed attention in the present moment, is said to place us in a tranquil condition that is known as *flow*.

Flow is a mode of hyper-awareness that's often intentionally accessed by athletes, musicians, artists, and other individuals who are aware of the power it yields to achieve an exceptional outcome and transform their experience.

When we're in flow, we're said to be *in the zone*, a psychological state that can influence our intellect, creativity, and physical performance, during which we're alert and focused in the moment.

Two examples of flow come to mind from my own experience. In the first, while in a tennis seminar, the instructor invited me to demonstrate a volleying technique we were just learning. I felt extreme anxiety to be demonstrating the technique to the other participants, which pushed me into a state of hyper-focus, and into the present. The intensity of the experience engulfed me. As I volleyed with the tennis pro, my mind perceived an expansion of time. All my senses were alerted. Soon I had an awareness that my attention was centered inside the tennis ball, and that my physical self was somehow connected to the ball. My muscles reacted with astounding precision.

My tennis ability in those minutes in flow far exceeded any actual skill I possessed either before or at any time after the event. Remarkably, many years later, my muscle memory of that occurrence remains clear.

In flow, time appears to speed up or slow down.

This phenomenon was even more amplified in a second example, when a vehicle in which I was a front-seat passenger was broadsided in an intersection. Moments before impact it felt as if time slowed to a crawl, and I became a witness to what was occurring. In an implausibly trance-like state I observed the passenger window beside me shatter, slow-motion, into thousands of pebbles that sprayed the vehicle's interior. It was only later, after I was pulled from the vehicle, that my perception of time returned to normal.

In both of my personal examples, and in other instances where being in the zone and experiencing flow have occurred in my life, the predominant feature has been concentrated and riveted attention that took charge of my anxiety while the event was taking place.

You may remember an instance when the stakes were extremely high, that the phenomenon of flow had an impact on an event.

Perhaps, you also remember a situation of lesser consequence, when a fragile object was knocked from a counter, slipped through your hands, and fell towards the floor.

Through some extraordinary feat of athleticism and coordination, in a stunning display, you caught the object mid-flight! Some aspect of your consciousness in those moments took charge of the event, focused your attention, and directed the outcome before your eyes.

I use these examples of flow to illustrate the extraordinary power of mindful attention.

Your thoughts create your reality.

Gaining mastery over our thoughts is a life-long pursuit. Despite our best efforts, we might be embarrassed about a remark we've made, or some action we've taken, feel anxious about an event, or suffer disappointment over some aspect of our self.

Sometimes it's difficult to remain in the moment, separate our process from the outcome, and keep up our spirits.

You are not your results!

During moments of panic or dread, all of us know what it's like to be socially awkward, complete with clammy palms and flop-sweat. Sometimes we fuss over unnecessary details, and are obsessed with gadgets. We've all had bad hair days and made clothing choices that are just wrong. We can be hyper-focused, tedious, and painfully dull.

At times we've cracked up at our own lame jokes, been blind to social cues, given long-winded explanations, and been entirely unaware that no one is even slightly interested in what we're talking about. Without question, all of us are nerdy.

Believe it. *Everyone* has nerdy parts. No matter how awesome and amazing another person appears, each and every day, they and everyone else fight a private battle with their own particular insecurities.

> When you embrace the nerd that you are, your act of self-acceptance raises your consciousness.

With self-acceptance, your self-esteem becomes shatter-proof, at least for the time being, and let's face it, the present moment is all there is.

> It's hard to take yourself seriously while affirming the brilliance of your nerd-dom.

On the following page you'll find the *Nerd Declaration*, a tool that will release you from self-judgment, cultivate your sense of humour, and assist you to lighten up.

The declaration of your nerd-dom is the ultimate strength contract and affirmation. Learn it!

Say it often:

I am a nerd.

I always was a nerd.

I always will be a nerd.

There is no hope.

wtf! I'm going for it anyway!

Chapter 4

YOUR FOCUS

Pay attention to yourself on purpose,
in the present moment, without judgment.

Who You Are

UP TO THIS POINT, you've explored the impact of fear and anxiety on the human brain, and you've discovered strategies you can employ to inspire your creativity and overcome habitual thought patterns and limitations.

From this point forward, the path you're on leads into a clearing.

Here, your focus is on *remembering* your strengths and affirming the reality of who you really are.

All of the parts of you; your experiences; your family history; your gender and birth order; the exposure you've had to art, culture, and education; the people you've encountered; your health and physical abilities; moments spent in nature; your connection to beloved pets, and wild things; instances of joy, and anguish, and heartbreak; creative sparks that have shaped you; challenges and risks that emboldened you; your place in time; stretches of playfulness; your memories; the learning journey you've embraced – every bit of the being that is you – all of this and more, together, has wrought the whole of you, and carved into the deepest parts of you your inner strengths, personal attributes, skills, accomplishments, achievements, interests, and your future hopes and dreams.

You are a singular, remarkable human. There's no one exactly like you. It's time for you to remember all of who you are, and for you to begin to think about the transferable nature of your strengths and qualities, and the enormous value that you contribute in your life, and that you bring to the world of work.

It's easy to get stuck here, in this place of strength, clarity, and illumination, mostly because the memories of being hurt, which are stored in the emotional brain, might feel under attack by your awakening inner strengths that have long been in the shadows.

Notice the ways you try to avoid moving forward through this chapter!

You'll need to rely heavily on your willingness to over-ride distractions — all forms of physical discomfort, including hunger, moments of annoyance, and especially feelings of fatigue. Notice your reactions, smile *(I am a nerd)*, and record your insights in your notebook.

There's extraordinary value for you to journal about the thoughts that are activated during these focussed exercises.

Stay in, and dig deep.

> ## Exchange habit for habit as you overcome your automatic thoughts, and *begin now* to predict your future success.

Write, record, jot down, and journal your thoughts. Then write some more.

Choose words and phrases that demonstrate how you're a *fit* for the job for which you want to apply.

Formulate a personal example of *how* and *when* you've demonstrated each strength, skill, and personal attribute. During interviews you'll be asked in countless different ways to give examples of your strengths and skills. That's not the best time for you to test your memory and sort through past experiences.

You'll send a powerful message when you match your strengths, skills, and attributes to the needs of the job for which you're applying. This is easy to accomplish – first think of the requirements of the job, and then reflect on instances when you've embodied those particular traits. Again, jot all of it down!

Strengths and Personal Attributes

I AM   *(choose and write down your personal attributes –
who you are)*

Choose at least 3 from the columns below, or substitute with
personal attributes that are not listed.

• Punctual	• Responsible	• Self-motivated
• Tidy	• Detail-oriented	• Willing to learn
• Curious	• Persistent	• People-oriented
• Organized	• Trustworthy	• Efficient
• Attentive	• Cooperative	• Eager
• Patient	• Friendly	• Persuasive
• Enthusiastic	• Quick learner	• Willing
• Careful	• Positive and helpful	• Good listener
• Health conscious	• Dependable	• Flexible
• Loyal	• Respectful	• Good communicator
• Considerate	• Confident	• Adaptable
• Creative	• Tolerant	• Resilient
• Appropriate	• Truthful	• Tenacious
• Forthright	• Capable	• Energetic
• Discerning	• Courageous	• Cool under pressure
• Kind	• Analytic	• Self-starter
• Sincere	• Collaborative	• Precise

A STRENGTH I HAVE: I AM ...

A STRENGTH I HAVE: I AM ...

A STRENGTH I HAVE: I AM ...

Skills

I HAVE THE FOLLOWING SKILLS
(write about what you have experience doing)

Choose 2 or 3 skills from the columns below, or substitute with skills that are not listed:

• Teamworking	• Effectively Communicating	• Cashiering
• Sales experience	• Technical ability	• Computer repairing
• Problem-solving	• Documenting	• Hosting
• Word processing	• Decision-making	• Managing social media
• Cooking and prepping	• Managing time	• Leadership
• Customer service	• Shipping	• Receiving
• Hands-on fixing, building	• Working under pressure	• Serving
• Self-managing	• Relationship building	• Researching
• Trouble-shooting	• Sorting, cataloguing	• Multi-tasking
• Bussing tables	• Speaking French	• Goal-setting
• Critical thinking	• Greeting customers	• Filing
• Automotive repair	• Having attention to detail	• Cataloguing

I AM SKILLED AT:

I AM SKILLED AT:

I AM SKILLED AT:

Accomplishments and Achievements

Search through your memories and write about your achievements with pride.

Use this list to prompt yourself and/or nudge your memory and make note of several of your accomplishments.

I AM PROUD THAT I:

- Have a Bronze Cross in swimming.
- Delivered newspapers 3 times a week for 2 years.
- Taught myself to play guitar.
- Graduated high school.
- Demonstrate kindness and cooperation.
- Earned a black belt in Tae Kwon Do.
- Quit smoking
- Babysit for neighbours and family.
- Cut and weed grandparents' lawn.
- Sang alone on stage.
- Volunteered at summer camp.
- Helped my father build a shed.
- Earned my airfare for a family trip
- Passed the exam for First Aid Level 2.
- Competed internationally on a ski team.

- Routinely cook dinner once a week for my family.
- Graduated after returning to school.
- Support myself after leaving home at 15.
- Lost 20 lbs. since last summer
- Play piano by ear.
- Tutor my sister who has an anxiety disorder.
- Work out routinely, and eat well.
- Have my driver's license.

I AM PROUD THAT I:

I AM PROUD THAT I:

I AM PROUD THAT I:

Interests

List the activities you enjoy or that you have a desire to try some day:

Choose 2 or 3. Explain how or why the activity interests you, or substitute with activities that are not on this list.

I AM INTERESTED IN

- Snowboarding
- Video gaming
- Cooking
- Singing
- Riding long board
- Listening to music
- Playing hockey

- Renovating
- Acting and rehearsing
- Playing guitar
- Mountain biking
- Working out

- Reading mysteries
- Building
- Travelling
- Cycling
- Popular culture

- Learning new things
- Watching movies

- Playing soccer
- Animal rescue

- Social media
- Studying languages
- Fixing things

- Baking
- Climbing
- Drawing
- Fishing
- Skiing

- Sewing

- Martial arts

- Researching
- Swimming

- Collecting
- Construction
- Painting and crafts

I HAVE AN INTEREST IN:

I HAVE AN INTEREST IN:

I HAVE AN INTEREST IN:

Future Hopes and Dreams

Use *action* words whenever you talk about your future hopes and dreams.

Choose 2 or 3 from this list, or substitute with some of your hopes and dreams that are not listed:

IN THE FUTURE I WANT TO:

- Drive a forklift
- Attend cooking school
- Become a firefighter
- Cheer at the Super Bowl
- Sky dive
- Hitchhike through Europe
- Start a business
- Speak in public
- Buy a condo
- Progress in my job
- Compete in a triathlon
- Repair cars
- Learn to cashier
- Be a builder/contractor
- Succeed at college
- Learn to drive a car
- Learn a language
- Play guitar
- Buy a car
- Graduate high school
- Travel to Asia
- Enter an apprenticeship
- Serve the public
- Start a family
- Design kitchens
- Grow within a career
- Train to be a florist
- Join the police or fire department

ONE OF MY DREAMS IS:

ONE OF MY DREAMS IS:

ONE OF MY DREAMS IS:

This chapter, *Chapter 4 – Your Focus*, has taken you on a journey through your past, your present, and your imagined future.

Whether you've found suitable examples from the lists provided, or you've opted for other words and phrases to describe your strengths, skills, accomplishments, achievements, interests, and your future hopes and dreams, the insight you've assembled with this inventory is substantial.

The best way to show what you can do, is to show what you can do.

In *Chapter 5 – Your Foundation*, which follows, you'll be asked to compose a resume.

Refer to the lists and the notes you've recorded in your notebook for assistance as you compile information for your resume.

You'll find that the list categories fit well into the functional resume style, which is most useful for first-time job seekers and people who are returning to the workforce after some time away.

Later, in *Chapter 5 – Your Foundation,* the lists in *Chapter 4 – Your Focus*, and your handwritten notations will help when you set out to formulate a comprehensive answer to *Can you tell me about yourself?*

Chapter 5

YOUR FOUNDATION

Let the process guide and inform you.

References

REFERENCE LISTS ARE COMPRISED of the names of people who will vouch for your work skills and experience, but most importantly, your reference people will affirm your character. They know who you are, because they've spent time with you, and they've observed an activity in which you've participated. Their willingness to give you a recommendation is based on respect you've earned. As you can imagine, not everyone is entitled to a reference.

Sometimes the people who act as a reference for you will write a letter of introduction that you can photocopy and bring with you to interviews. Most of the time, though, employers will check your references through a phone call or by email contact.

Application forms typically ask for the names of two or more references, along with their contact information – their email addresses and phone numbers. Prior to attending an interview, you're encouraged to prepare an *application form template*, which is explained later in this chapter.

You'll include the names of your reference people on the application form template, along with how to reach them.

Take a moment to give your references a heads-up so they're aware they might be contacted to speak on your behalf.

It's helpful to let them know the skills required of the particular job for which you're a candidate, so they can adjust their remarks about your strengths in those particular skill areas.

Certificates and Diplomas

If you've received any awards, citations, commendations, certificates, diplomas, letters of accomplishment, or other tributes to your character and achievements, photocopy and place the copies in a large manila envelope. Take the envelope with you to the interview. You'll have some time before the interview to reflect on your accomplishments. These copies will be useful memory prompts and confidence builders for you at that time.

In the event a topic which touches on one of your achievements arises during the interview, you'll have a certificate to present to the interviewer that highlights that accomplishment.

Your Resume

Since your aim is to be hired, throughout the entire interview process it's important for you to stand out from your competitors for the position.

> ## Your objective is to present yourself in the best light possible, starting with a solid resume and cover letter.

Finding a resume template is easy. Search online for *youth resumes*, *entry-level job resumes*, and *functional resumes*, any of which should be suitable for first-time or entry-level job interviews. If you've interviewed in the past and you already have a work history, search online for *chronological resumes*, which is a format that might better fit your needs.

Your resume should provide a quick narrative of your skills and attributes. Keep your functional resume simple, all on one page, and strive in the resume to give a confident and accurate account of your strengths, accomplishments, goals, interests, and experiences.

A chronological resume that's expanded to two or more pages is a *curriculum vitae*, known as a C.V., a document that provides a formal summary of a candidate's professional skills and experience.

A career professional who's returning to the workforce in their field will typically use a C.V. in place of a resume. The C.V. requires a formal presentation and will usually be prepared by a career coach or resume writing service.

As you develop your resume from an online template or from examples in a job finding workshop or book, use the answers you've harvested in *Chapter 4, Your Focus* to guide you, along with other information found in this book.

Application Form Template

Many restaurant chains, grocers, and service-oriented businesses conduct interviews without formal appointments. For example, a restaurant might accept drop-in interviews on specific days between certain hours.

If you want to be sure of the particulars of the company's drop-in interview times, call the business phone line, or check the company's website for details.

When you arrive during the drop-in interview period, you'll likely be handed an application form to complete. In a drop-in scenario, it's common for several people to be waiting to be interviewed, all filling out application forms at the same time.

You're essentially in a queue. It's first-come, first-served, and you'll want to arrive early to be among the first people interviewed, before the interview team is fatigued.

Since all of your actions are on display when you're applying for a job, speed and efficiency matter. You won't want to appear slow-moving, even though you're just filling out an application form!

When your application form is complete, immediately submit it to the customer service desk, restaurant host, or greeter, and wait your turn to be interviewed.

Filling out a job application form requires focus and a good deal of information. It can be a daunting and discouraging process if you don't have the information on hand that you're asked to supply on the form, especially when your attention could be better focused on relaxing and remaining confident, rather than worrying about remembering details for the application form.

Most importantly, struggling to remember dates, locations, supervisors' names, and contact information for your references will sabotage your efforts and scatter your energy.

A winning strategy is to fill out a *job application template* when you're composing your resume.

There are never surprises on application forms, and standard application forms are easily found online. Download and print out an application, or visit a large specialty warehouse store or fast-food franchise and obtain their form. Whichever method you use to obtain a paper application, it will be a valuable template for filling out future job applications.

Take time at home to carefully record your answers to every question on the application form.

Don't leave any blank space. For instance, if you've never worked before, and you're asked to list your previous employers, indicate *N/A* or print *not applicable.* Or you can indicate in that space: *This will be my first job*. Or specify, *This was a volunteer position*, and list the name of the organization and appropriate details, with the same amount of consideration as if the volunteer listing was a paid position.

The point is, don't leave blank spaces on your application template, or on any application form that you complete. If you leave spaces, the assumption is that for some reason you've intentionally omitted important information, which could take you out of the running for an interview.

Always provide correct spelling and punctuation.

Ensure that you carefully print (not write) the information on your template. Although the application template will not be seen by anyone else, neatness counts.

The carefully filled-out template may help you later to remember to keep the actual application form as neat as possible when you're copying from your template to the job application form, oftentimes just before your interview.

Your job application template is a valuable tool that should be with you every time you attend a job interview, along with:

- a pen that has sufficient ink, and a back-up pen, just in case;
- two copies of your updated resume; and
- photocopies of any certificates or awards you've earned.

Successful companies value attention to detail in their employees.

The job interview provides an excellent opportunity for you to show the interviewer that you're aware of the importance of such attention to detail.

In all, your professional-looking resume, the comments you make in the interview demonstrating that you've researched the company, and the ease of your conversation with the interviewer, taken together, will leave a positive impression and indicate your preparedness and your respect for attention to detail.

Online Applications

Commonly today applications are submitted online in the hospitality, service, specialty and warehouse, and retail sectors.

It's just as important to pay attention to spelling and punctuation in an online application, and to carefully answer all of the questions asked. These elements give subtle cues about your attention to detail.

Online applications may include a questionnaire that asks you to consider specific situations and respond in your own words in short answers, in addition to a section of multiple-choice questions.

If the website allows you to print your completed online application and questionnaire, it's a good idea to print and save it for later review. If you're invited to attend an interview, a question or two from your online questionnaire might be referred to in your interview, so it's always good to review your answers in advance of that meeting.

Wait a week to receive a response to an online application. If you haven't heard back by then, phone the manager or assistant manager of the store, restaurant, or service agency, to enquire about the status of your application.

A courteous follow-up enquiry about the status of your online application can open the door to an invitation for an interview.

Immediately following each telephone or in-person contact, remember to record the name of the person to whom you have spoken, and refer to that person by name, in any later telephone calls as well as at your interview.

If you're told during your follow-up call that the position has been filled, take that opportunity to ask if your application will be brought forward during the next hiring period. If not, make a calendar note to reapply in a month or six weeks' time.

The Core Interview Question: Can You Tell Me About Yourself?

The point of the job interview is for the person who's interviewing you to get to know you and assess your suitability for a particular job. They'll ask you questions about your strengths, interests, goals, and other basic information to help them discover who you are.

In order to find out about you, interviewers often lead with some variation of the question *Can you tell me about yourself?*

The question is code for:

Who are you?

What's important to you? and

Why are <u>you</u> the best person for the job?

Your response to the question *Can you tell me about yourself?* is the best way to let the interviewer know that you're the perfect person to fill the job for which they're hiring.

If you haven't yet composed your casual and professional responses to *Can you tell me about yourself?* go back to the *Communication* section in *Chapter 2,* and with *Chapter 4* also in mind, prepare a first draft of your best answers to *Can you tell me about yourself?* and record your answers in your notebook.

Over time, as you continue to work through these pages and become more comfortable acknowledging your strengths and other attributes, your job interview answer to *Can you tell me about yourself?* will grow into a more natural and confident reply.

Your answer is a work in progress. Keep refining it.

Your answer should be brief, like an *elevator pitch*, which is comprised of a few sentences that you would be able to deliver during a short elevator ride, of one minute or less.

This aspect of your interview can be seamless. All that's required is for you to prepare and practice a script that contains your own authentic statements, following the example in the template below:

When your interviewer asks: *Can you tell me about yourself?*

- Smile. And start with:

  I'd be glad to. As you know, my first name is _____.

  It's useful to state your name at this point, in case the interviewer has forgotten.

- Tell them why you're applying for the job, for example:

  Although I'm new to looking for employment, I've assessed my qualifications and I've researched the types of jobs that are a good fit for my skills.

- Tell them two or three of your personal characteristics, for example:

  I'm an eager learner. I'm curious, and I like to fix things.

- Give an example of something you've accomplished, for example:

  I've volunteered at the Food Bank for over a year now, and recently I graduated high school with an almost perfect attendance record. Last year my soccer team competed for the Provincial Cup. I studied music all through school and I currently play guitar in a band.

- Tell them why you'd be excellent for this job, for example:

  I am detail-oriented, I can focus for long periods of time, and one of my strongest attributes is reliability.

- Give them your closing statement:

  I would be an asset to your organization, since your company values teamwork and customer service, which are two of my strengths.

To give you a sense how the answer to *Can you tell me about yourself?* would be delivered in an actual interview, the sentences would follow one after the other, in this way:

As you know, my first name is _____. Although I'm new to looking for employment, I've assessed my qualifications and I've researched the types of jobs that are a good fit for my skills.

I'm an eager learner. I'm curious, and I like to fix things. I've volunteered at the Food Bank for over a year now, and recently I graduated high school with an almost perfect attendance record.

Last year my soccer team competed for the Provincial Cup. I studied music all through school, and I currently play guitar in a band.

I am detail-oriented, I can focus for long periods of time, and one of my strongest attributes is reliability.

I would be an asset to your organization, since your company values teamwork and customer service, which are two of my strengths.

With practice you'll become comfortable and give natural responses.

Ultimately, how you choose to tell the interviewer about yourself will play a large part in whether or not you land the job.

The impression you give might even have an impact on the wages you're offered. The stakes are high.

> When you prepare and practice, your responses will reflect the effort you've put in.

Typical Interview Questions

Long before you attend a job interview you'll have engaged in extensive preparation and spent time practicing and rehearsing your answers to questions the interviewer might ask, so you'll be conditioned, and able to think on your feet.

The interviewer might give you some questions around a *specific situation*, and ask how *you've used a particular skill* or *reached an outcome*, or *handled a situation* in the past. What they're asking is for you to *draw on your memory* of a particular event *and give particulars about your actual behaviours and actions*.

Another type of interview question is also focused on a situation, but in this case, the *situation or scenario is specific to the job for which you're being interviewed*.

Since it's likely you *haven't encountered that specific situation*, and you *haven't done the job before*, your answers are meant to reveal *how you would assess the situation* and *reach a solution,* or *problem-solve*.

On the following pages you'll find a number of questions that are frequently asked in job interviews.

Think about each question. Take your time.

Be authentic.

Answer truthfully.

In your notebook, write out each question. Think about concrete examples from your own experience (something you've actually done, whether at home or in your personal life, at school, or in a previous job). If you haven't had experience with a specific situation, *imagine* for each question how you'd respond, if the scenarios actually occurred.

Record your answers in your notebook so you can review, revise, and expand on them later.

As often as you can, practice your answers to each of the questions with someone. Whenever you practice, whether alone or with another person, answer the questions fully, and out loud, so you can actually hear how you've worded your responses, and adjust, if necessary.

Smile, and speak with enthusiasm even when you practice.

Allow your face to be animated when you answer the questions, both during your practice sessions, and in an actual interview.

Personalize your answers with phrases like the following:

I am...
When I...
In the past I have...
In the future I...

The prompts that are found below each of the example interview questions are provided as *suggestions*, and merely scratch the surface of possible responses.

In any case, formulate your answers to the questions in a way that reflects *your* particular views. *Give examples* in your responses, and challenge yourself to *answer in full sentences.*

Be sure to keep your answers interesting, and use a well-rounded vocabulary.

What can you tell me about yourself?

You will always be asked this question in a job interview, usually in addition to a number of other questions, similar to the ones suggested here. Sometimes a version of Can you tell me about yourself? is the only question you will be asked in the interview. That is how important your answer is! For guidance in preparing your answer to What can you tell me about yourself? see the Can you tell me about yourself? script above.

How would others who know you describe you?

Think about a positive experience you've had with a favourite teacher, your best friend, a grandparent, your significant other, and how they would speak about you. He is determined, good-natured, helpful, a natural leader.

What is your greatest strength or strengths?

From your list of strengths, choose those that are complementary to the job you want. In order to best respond to this question, you should spend some time before the interview researching the tasks required in the particular job, as well as the requirements of the specific company or organization for which you're applying.

What are some of your weaknesses?

Balance your strengths and weaknesses in your mind, and consider the benefits of each strength and weakness in your life. For example, in a job that requires you to field telephone queries and complaints, you might let the interviewer know, I tend to take time to look at both sides of an issue which might briefly add to the decision-making process, but on the other hand, people have told me they appreciate that I am diplomatic and fair. My qualities are strengths for a person who is working on a help desk.

What trait or traits of your parent(s) would you like to bring forward in your life, and why?

This is a great opportunity for you to express admiration for your parent(s), and respect for their attributes. This question is a powerful indication that this employer is driven by strong human values. If corporate ethics and human issues are significant to you, you're interviewing with a great potential employer for you. Explore this answer in advance. It might be the eventual response to a different question entirely, and an opening for you to reveal to your interviewer the depth of your insight. For example, My Dad always takes the time to acknowledge when someone is helpful, and I can see how his words make a difference to others.

What is an example of your leadership?

When have you led others? Think about your relationships with siblings, sports team members, church groups, classmates, and times you took a stand, or in some way exercised your leadership.

In what situations have you been a leader?

Give examples of actual situations, what happened, and the outcome. As an example, As I was driving along a narrow roadway, a bicycle riding on the shoulder of the road approached from the opposite direction. The bicycle wheels slid in the gravel and the rider crashed and hit his head. I pulled my car to the roadside, put on my 4-way flashers, waved the car behind me to pull over. I immediately dialed 9-1-1 and called for an ambulance. I directed the other vehicle driver to help keep the cyclist warm. I took charge of the situation, calmed the cyclist, and kept him conscious until the EMTs arrived.

What kind of a leader are you?

Leadership comes in all shapes and sizes. Some leaders are seen as considerate, some are tough. Some are collaborative, and some are directive. The best leaders are flexible in their approach and lead according to the situation.

How do you typically follow a leader?

In other words, what is your usual 'follower' style? Do you give input, ask questions, offer respect and loyalty? Is your follower style all of the above, or something different?

To what groups, if any, do you belong?

You may belong to an organized group, such as a sailing club, act as a volunteer to a Wildlife Rescue, or maybe you've signed on as a member of a soccer or other athletic team (player, coach). Or alternatively, you might informally spend time in an online group, occasionally run at a local track, or perhaps root for a local sports team. Use your personal examples.

What makes a good team player?

Think about the qualities you have that make you a sought-after friend and companion: committed, reliable and responsible, respectful, flexible.

How do you spend your leisure time?

Expand your answer to consider each season of the year. Perhaps sometimes you are with others, alone, dog-walking, volunteering, reading, hiking, going to the gym.

Why are your leisure time activities important to you?

Your best answers will provide the interviewer with a window into the person you are, so give a rounded view. For example: My leisure activities are an opportunity for me to interact with others, they provide balance, and lift my mood.

Where do you see yourself within five years?

Answer briefly, both personally and professionally, and as with all of your answers, give a full and balanced view of yourself. For example: Within five years, I see myself living in a condo downtown, training for a supervisory position, travelling on vacation, and attending night classes to advance my career.

What are your goals/ dreams/ambitions?

Think long-term (10 years) and short-term (up to 5 years), and give a sampling of your future self. For example: In the short term I want to develop myself professionally, and longer-term I'd like to get married and start a family, and somewhere in there, complete my degree.

What is your learning style?

In other words, how do you learn best? (Through your eyes, ears, hands.)

With an entry-level job, it is useful to say that: I like to be shown how to do something, and be given a chance to try it out to show the person who is training me, be corrected if necessary, and then demonstrate my ability again.

How would a former teacher describe you?

Here's another opportunity for you to confidently talk about the wonderful parts of you. For example: My English teacher would say I am helpful, eager, respectful, and I can be counted on to do what I say I'll do.

What do you do when you forget an instruction?

At some point, everyone has forgotten an instruction, so there's no need to be shy or to hold back your answer. Some examples are: I'd ask to be reminded; I'd speak with my supervisor and let them know I've forgotten their instruction; I'd confer with a co-worker and ask them to show and tell me.

What do you do when you make a mistake?

Be honest. Everyone makes mistakes! You need not be shy with this answer either. You might say: I'd try to sort it out the best I can but first I'd let my supervisor know, just to make sure nothing goes wrong.

How do you ask for help?

In other words, are you direct, or indirect? Think about a couple of personal examples. What do you tend to do when you need help? What do you say?

How do you respond under stress?

In this regard, everyone is somewhat different. Some people seem to manage stress in the moment, without any obvious struggle. Others become rattled and may even be irritable. There is a range of possibilities. No matter what, it's important to remain mindful when times are tough. You might let your interviewer know that under stress you aim for balance, and try to stay connected with others. For example: When I'm stressed I try to take some time alone; I'd ask for support; I'd discuss my concerns with my supervisor.

How do you respond in new situations?

In new situations people tend to feel like fish out of water. In other words, uncomfortable, with a strong desire to return to what is familiar. Your interviewer wants to know how resilient you will be when you're faced with change. You must answer truthfully to this, and any interview question, being aware that when you're mindful you're in a position to choose how you will respond. Examples of possible answers to this question are: I'd proceed cautiously and make sure I have all the information I need; I'd trust myself and know that everything will work out; I'd jump in right away. I love change!

Can you work under pressure?

Be sure not to give a simple 'yes' answer. Here's another opportunity for you to reflect on the past – think about a high-stakes family or seasonal event, a school activity, some clock-ticking sports competition, a public performance, or any other challenge you've encountered. Then give an example of a time you completed a task or project, or succeeded in some way, despite being under stress.

How would you handle a conflict with a co-worker?

As with any stressful situation, being in conflict with a co-worker is challenging. Think about how you've handled conflict in the past. Some examples of ways to manage conflict include: I'd ignore it – let bygones be bygones; I'd speak with the co-worker and try to resolve the issue; I'd discuss the problem with my supervisor.

How do you react to criticism?

There are benefits to all forms of feedback. Don't be limited by the following examples. Some possible answers to this question are: I'd listen to the person who is critiquing me or my actions, and try to understand where they are coming from. I'd thank them for their feedback, and let them know I'll try to learn from their comments.

What would you do if you're dealing with a customer who is rude to you?

The interviewer wants you to indicate the specific actions you would take, even though you may never have encountered the situation in a workplace. Here you can draw from random times when someone has been rude to you. Some examples are: I'd remain polite; I'd do my best to defuse the situation; I'd advise my supervisor if the situation escalates.

If you noticed a customer or co-worker stealing, what would you do?

Again, although you might never have encountered a situation like this, the interviewer wants you to indicate the specific hypothetical actions you would take, so they can get a sense of your instincts. Answer from your gut. Here are some likely responses: I'd advise my supervisor immediately; I'd keep an eye on the individual but not get involved; In the case of a customer, I'd inform another staff member.

How would you handle impatient shoppers when you're on the job?

Think about how you respond to impatient people in general, and indicate the specific actions you would take. For example: I'd attempt to smooth over the situation, acknowledge the unfortunate situation, apologize, and keep my cool.

What would you do if a restaurant guest complains about their meal?

Most restaurant hosts and servers are trained that the guest is always right, and servers are expected to respond to such a complaint with empathy. As an example: I'd ask the guest if I can get them a replacement meal, apologize, and let the restaurant manager know so they can deal with the problem. (Typically restaurant managers deduct the cost of the meal from the bill.)

How would you support our company's mission and goals?

You could talk about your personal strengths and how you see those strengths benefiting the company. For example: This company's mission is to provide customer service that makes a difference. I am a good listener and I can be counted on to do my best to make my customers my priority.

What do you know about this company?

Research the company online so you can state the company's objectives and mission, and their reputation in the community. For example, This auto repair shop is committed to friendly, first-rate service, at the best price. I remember when I was in the first grade my Dad brought me here to pick up our car. We watched Tony finish off the brake job, and Tony let me push the lever to lower the car from the hoist. That was the day I decided I wanted to be an automotive mechanic.

Please state our company's mission in your own words.

Having researched the company online, you can talk about what you know about their public reputation and the way they do business. For example: This supermarket's prices are lower and at least in line with their competitors, but I think the most significant aspect to your success is the service that you provide to your customers, from the workers who stock the shelves to the cashiers and bagging helpers. Everyone gives great service and that word has spread throughout the community.

Why should we hire you?

Here's an opportunity to re-state your Can you tell me about yourself? script. Don't hold back. They might have missed it the first time!

and

Why should we hire you over someone else with the same qualifications?

Think about the skills and qualities the company is looking for, and give examples of your strengths that fit their needs. You can even re-state your Can you tell me about yourself? script:

I'm an eager learner. I'm curious, and I like to fix things. I've volunteered at the Food Bank for over a year now, and recently I graduated high school with an almost perfect attendance record.

Last year my soccer team competed for the Provincial Cup. I studied music all through school, and I currently play guitar in a band.

I am detail-oriented, I can focus for long periods of time, and one of my strongest attributes is reliability.

I would be an asset to your organization, since your company values teamwork and customer service, which are two of my strengths.

Why do you want to work here?

Talk about your personal strengths and how you see those strengths benefiting the company. For example:

This company has a great reputation for providing first-class customer service. I am a good listener and I can be counted on to do my best. I'll make my customers my priority, and get satisfaction from doing a good job with a company that I am proud to work for.

Why do you want this particular job?

Talk about your attributes and how the job is a perfect fit for you. For example:

I am _____, _____, and _____. I am eager to learn everything I can about _____, and this opportunity excites me. For as long as I can remember I have wanted to _____. I see this job as a great chance to get started on this career path.

What would cause you to miss a work shift?

Stand out from the crowd. Hopefully you can say: I'm the kind of person who shows up no matter what. If I'm sick you can send me home.

How will you get to work and home?

Don't let logistics bog you down. If you have a car, state it. If you take transit, state it. Travel to and from work should not be an issue. For example: I have a car. I live close to transit.

When are you available to start work?

Answer with enthusiasm: As soon as possible!

Near the end of the interview when the interviewer asks, *Do you have any questions for me?* be sure to have at least two questions prepared to ask them.

If the interviewer *hasn't* asked if you have questions, and you notice the interview is winding down, you can say, *I have a couple of questions for you. Is this a good time for me to ask you?*

The questions you ask should be *specific to the company*, and should show that you've researched and put forth effort preparing them.

It's best to ask *what* and *how* questions, and stay away from asking, *why?*

> Avoid asking the interviewer questions that could be answered *yes* or *no,* because they can lead to dead-end responses which could make the situation awkward and confusing for you.

The most *suitable* questions you can ask are those that indicate that *you're curious about the job and the company*, and might include the following:

- What qualities should I have, in order to succeed at this job?
- Can you tell me about the tasks I'd be doing?
- Where would I find material to read about the job I'd be doing?

If you feel comfortable asking the interviewer questions that are more personal, you might consider the following:

- What steps did you take to get to your position in the company?
- What do you like best about working for this company?
- What are the next steps that will happen at your end after this interview?

- What steps would you suggest I take now in order to be considered for the job?

And be sure to let the interviewer know:

- I'll call in several days to follow up. How should I remind you about me and my interview?

Later, when you land the job, you can ask questions about your salary and benefits; what, if any safety equipment, special clothing or particular shoes you'll require, and all of the specific details about reporting for work.

CHAPTER 6

THE JOB INTERVIEW PROCESS

Stay the course.
From starting gate to finish line, details matter.

Job Seeking Tasks

ALTHOUGH YOUR PARTICULAR CIRCUMSTANCES may vary, below are basic job-seeking tasks, from the particular *motivating factor* that started the process for you, all the way to accepting the position.

The job search process is complex, for which you'll need to multi-task and utilize among other talents, your:

- research abilities;
- communication and writing skills;
- organizing aptitude; and
- attention to detail.

An example of a *motivating factor* is that you want to earn money for school. So then...

- You narrow down your employment choices, and think about options.

- You consider your strengths, abilities, previous experiences, and interests.

- Specific job options that suit your profile come into view.

- You target employment possibilities in those areas for which you feel suited.

- You research how to write a resume and cover letter, and you prepare them.

- You create an application form template and record all necessary details.

- You fill out job applications online and in person.

- You follow up and remind employers that you're eager to be interviewed.

- You respond to an invitation to attend an interview at a specific date and time and confirm your attendance.

- You record the details of the invitation phone call or email for future reference.

- You practice answering typical interview questions.

- You prepare your clothing for the interview.

- You decide on the best travel option to get to your interview location.

- You go to bed early the evening before your interview.

- You dress and groom yourself appropriately.

- You ensure you have eaten and had sufficient water before your interview.

- You arrive on time.

- You introduce yourself to the greeter or receptionist.

- You keep your focus in the interview and give it your best.

- You email or mail a thank-you note to your interviewer.

- You follow up several days later.

- You receive word on the outcome.

- You accept the job offer!

Clothing Guidelines and Choices

Throughout your interview preparation, keep in mind that your grooming and clothing choices are leading factors in determining your success in landing the job.

When you attend an interview, you'll want to fit in, and appear as if you already work for the company. Make it easy for the interviewer to imagine you as their employee.

You can accomplish this if you conduct a bit of research beforehand to establish the company dress code and norms, including the colour palette, if they have one.

The dress code is easy to check out when you apply for a position in a retail store, restaurant, coffee shop, or other accessible worksite. If the company's employees wear a uniform, your best option is to dress in the colours of the company's uniform. The interviewer will notice that you're paying attention.

If it's difficult to pay a visit to the company due to location, security, or privacy concerns, don't be shy about making a telephone call to the company's main telephone number.

Mention to the person answering the call that you'll be attending a job interview and ask how employees at the company dress for that specific job. Then pull together interview clothing that follows that standard.

Keep Your Clothing Choices Simple.

Take care to gather your interview attire well in advance of your scheduled meeting. Check for missing buttons, torn hems, marks and stains, and proceed accordingly.

Even a little bit of discomfort with your shoes or clothing is guaranteed to deflate your confidence in an interview situation, where it's likely your level of self-consciousness will already be high.

Before purchasing any clothing items for an interview, check with friends and family members to see if they have what you need. Later, if you land the job, you can invest in clothing essentials for your work. For now, borrowed is good.

Interview Clothing Rules for Entry-Level Service and Trades Jobs that Should Never Be Broken

Never wear leggings to a job interview.

Never wear jogging pants, athletic pants, yoga pants, or shorts to a job interview unless you're applying for a job in a gym.

Never wear jeans with slashed knees, rips, or tears to a job interview.

Never wear low cut tops or revealing clothing to a job interview.

Never wear a tank top or sleeveless undershirt to a job interview.

Never wear a t-shirt with graphics to a job interview.

Never wear a hoodie to a job interview.

Never wear a baseball cap, knit cap, or toque to a job interview unless you're applying for a job on a ski hill or in a bicycle sales and repair shop.

Remove piercings. At the interview you can mention that you have piercings and ask about the company policy.

Long hair should be in a bun or knot, or tied back.

Minimal make-up.

Minimal jewelry. Men should not wear heavy wrist or neck chains.

Shoes should always be flat, with no open toes.

A jacket should always be worn or with you, unless it's a hot summer day.

Although street wear and casual attire – yoga pants, tank tops, leggings, jogging pants, and hoodies – are now common-place, neither street wear nor casual attire are acceptable clothing choices to wear when dropping off application forms, or for attending a job interview, no matter how casual or informal the setting might be. And no matter what anyone else has told you.

Interview Clothing Suggestions for Specific Jobs

Animal care – jeans or cotton slacks, t-shirt or collared long-sleeved shirt or blouse, casual shoes

Automotive – jeans, t-shirt or collared long-sleeved shirt or blouse, dark runners or work boots

Bakery – white long-sleeved shirt or black or white t-shirt, dark pants, casual shoes or runners

Bike shop, ski shop – jeans or cotton slacks, t-shirt, runners or casual shoes

Coffee shop – white or black long-sleeved shirt or t-shirt, black pants, casual shoes

Construction – jeans, dark t-shirt, runners, work boots, or casual shoes

Dollar store – white or neutral long-sleeved shirt or blouse, dark pants, casual shoes

Fast food – white long-sleeved shirt or blouse or white t-shirt, dark pants, casual shoes

Grocery store – long-sleeved shirt or blouse, jacket, dark pants, casual shoes

Gym or community centre – athletic pants, dark t-shirt, runners

Hospitality, hotel – white or black collared shirt or blouse, jacket, black dress pants, black shoes.

Spa – white long-sleeved shirt or blouse, black pants, black shoes

Landscaper – jeans, t-shirt, dark runners, work boots, or casual shoes

Lumber and hardware retailer – jeans or casual pants, collared shirt, dark runners or work boots

Movie theatre – white or neutral long-sleeved shirt or blouse, dark pants, casual shoes

Office and professional – dark suit and tie/jacket, white or pastel shirt or blouse, dress shoes

Pizza restaurant – white or black t-shirt, dark jeans or pants, casual shoes

Restaurant – white collared shirt or blouse, black pants, black shoes

Retail – white or neutral long-sleeved shirt or blouse, dark dress pants or skirt, black shoes

Service – white long-sleeved shirt or blouse, dark dress pants, black shoes

Swamping, delivery – jeans, dark t-shirt, runners or work boots

After you're hired, you can follow whatever company norms apply, but at the application form and interview stages it's important not to make assumptions about what's acceptable. It's better to err on the side of caution.

The Information Interview

If you want first-hand information about a particular job in which you have an interest pursuing, an information interview is an excellent way to gather the inside details.

As a first step, do a bit of research to determine the best person with whom to meet. When you have decided who that person is, call the company and obtain his or her email address.

Compose a brief email requesting a fifteen-minute meeting to conduct an interview with them to gather information. You should stress that you're not seeking employment, but are looking for information to assist you in determining your future career direction. If they respond favourably to your request, set a time, and prepare your questions.

Information interviews in the *service, hospitality, retail, construction, trades,* and *automotive* sectors tend to be casual in nature, and rarely exceed *fifteen minutes* in length. There's a chance you'll be standing during the interview, in an area where business is conducted, often with customers present.

In *office, sales,* and *professional* settings, information interviews are typically conducted in a private office or in an area away from clients and employees. Information interviews in these settings tend to range from *fifteen to thirty minutes* in length.

Make a point to arrive ten minutes early for your information interview, suitably dressed, with a number of questions you've prepared. If you're uncertain about appropriate attire for the interview, refer to the information listed above under the heading *Interview Clothing Suggestions for Specific Jobs.*

Questions for the information interview should focus on a specific job for which you have an interest, the skill level, training, and experience required to do the job, typical employment opportunities in the field, pro's and con's, and any advice the person you're interviewing can give you about entering that particular field.

During the information interview, it's your responsibility to lead the discussion, and you should be ready to ask questions that you've prepared and brought with you.

Keep your eye on the time. Unless you're gathering information for an office or professional job, wrap up within the fifteen-minute time period.

In any case, if the person you're interviewing appears to be rushed or distracted, ask your most pertinent questions, keep the energy moving, and conclude the interview early on a high note.

Initiate closure by extending your hand for a handshake, thank them for their time, and leave.

As soon as you're able, compose and send a brief email with *Thank you* in the subject line, similar to this example:

> *Dear _____,*
> *Thank you for spending time with me today and answering my questions about _____. You have given me a lot to think about, and I am grateful for all of your suggestions and information!*
> *Regards, _____*

Information interviews are an excellent way for you to gather insight into a job within a particular field, to get a sense of current and future opportunities, and to explore the major employers in that field. Asking for information will give you first-hand experience, and the entire process can be a confidence builder. Visiting varied workplaces offers a window into the ways in which organizations do business, and provides you with a sense of the other side of the desk, that you can call on when you prepare for future job interviews.

There's no limit to the number of information interviews you can conduct in any field, and although it's best not to return to speak to someone else in the same company for at least three months, the sky is the limit if you decide to query varied organizations in the same or other areas of interest.

Leading Up to The Job Interview

- At least two days before your job interview, launder, iron, and prepare your clothing and shoes.
- Assemble your documents - application template, 2 copies of your resume, and 2 reliable pens.
- Determine your transit route, or confirm the parking availability if you'll be driving.
- The night before the interview, ensure that you get to bed early and have plenty of sleep.
- The day of the interview, pay attention to grooming – nails, hair, beard.
- Make sure to eat and drink water prior to the interview.
- Keep yourself calm – use positive imaging and self-talk.

What to Take to the Interview

- A zippered case or satchel to hold your documents and pens;
- Two pens; (One is a back-up, just in case.)
- Two copies of your resume in a large brown envelope; (One copy for you, one for your interviewer.)
- Two copies of your reference page;

- Pre-filled application form to use as a template;
- Copies of your certificates or letters of accomplishment in a separate brown envelope;
- Your notebook;
- Neatly written questions about the specific job and the company that you can refer to at the end of the interview when your interviewer asks if you have any questions;
- Directions/transit information to the interview;
- Company telephone number (so you can call to postpone in case an emergency occurs while you're on your way).

CHAPTER 7

THE JOB INTERVIEW –
YOUR BEST FOOT FORWARD

Don't focus on you. This is bigger than you.
Focus on the value of what you have to offer.

.

When You Arrive for the Interview

SHOW UP EARLY. Arrive at the interview location ten or fifteen minutes before you're scheduled to meet. Give yourself plenty of time so you have a few minutes to visit the washroom and freshen up.

Check in with the person at the front desk. Ask the receptionist or greeter for your interviewer's business card, or a card with the company's address and phone number.

If the front desk greeter doesn't have a business card for the person who'll interview you, ask for the spelling of your interviewer's first and last names, their job title, and email address, and jot it down. After the interview you'll use this information to send a thank you email, and several days to a week later, you'll use it to conduct your interview follow up.

Have your pen ready. You could be asked to fill out an application form, or another document prior to your interview.

Transfer the information from the application form template you filled out at home and brought with you.

From the time you and the others who are competing for the same job arrive for your interviews, everything any of you do is on display. Your interviewer might ask the front desk greeter, concierge, security officer, or receptionist how you interacted with them, how you treated others, how you spent your time waiting, and if you were patient as you waited. The rules of etiquette and polite behaviour always apply.

There's an old saying that cautions, *you don't get a second chance to make a first impression.*

When you arrive at the waiting area, until you leave the premises, turn your phone off or put it in airplane mode. Turn off any electronic devices and keep them out of sight in a bag, purse, or briefcase. At such an important time, focusing on your gadgets can pull you out of the moment.

Resist the urge to sneak a peek at your phone or to put any attention at all on the device, even if you feel your anxiety spike, and you're extraordinarily compelled to pull out your phone and check it.

Resisting the urge to refer to your screens will keep your mind on the upcoming interview, and allow you time to prepare and reflect.

You relay a strong message about your maturity and your commitment to the entire interview process when you remain present. This gives you an advantage over applicants who are unaware of how their actions and behaviours before and after the actual interview impact the outcome.

Use your waiting time wisely. Read over documents you've brought with you, to refresh your thoughts. Review your resume, and wait quietly for the interviewer to call on you.

In the minutes just before the interviewer is about to meet with you, your task is to quiet your mind, pull your thoughts into the present, and affirm your strengths. *This is a great time to utilize your strength contract!*

The following imagination exercise is intended to focus your attention and enhance your energy. Practice this at home, so that you're comfortable with the breathing aspect, and you can do the exercise without bringing attention to yourself.

The focus helps to relax and bring you into the present. It's useful to run through the exercise just before you're called to go into the interview.

> *Sit quietly, place your attention in your eyes, and breathe slowly and intentionally.*

Imagine that your energy, that invisible field that surrounds you, expands due to the intensity of your attention. When you focus your attention in the moment you increase the amount of energy you transmit.

Now direct all of your attention into the space right behind your eyes. Feel the force of your energy build as your eyes infuse with energy.

Notice your breathing. Pull the air in through your nose, all the way into your lungs. Breathe out slowly; breathe in again, and slowly out. Feel how present you are.

Practice softening your gaze, while you remain in the moment, fully charged and present.

The Job Interview Explained

A job interview is an opportunity for you to tell your story to someone who wants to know about your strengths and attributes, and the value you bring to the situation.

Your story should be the best possible version of the truth about you.

Interviews are a process. Most people never think about what the interview process will actually entail, and they aren't prepared to present who they are to their best advantage in a job interview.

The average entry-level job interview is thirty minutes long. Some interviews are shorter, and sometimes an interview runs longer, especially interviews for jobs that provide service to the public, including most retail and sales positions, and interviews for jobs that require prior experience and technical expertise.

As you advance in your work life, you'll experience a variety of interview formats. Circumstances vary widely, according to the field of work, geographical location, cultural and social norms, and a candidate's credentials, experience, and expertise.

Regardless of the format, you'll enter the interview at the start of the process; immerse yourself in the interview and move through it; and then the interview will conclude and you'll leave the process.

Interviews have typical beginnings: You and your interviewer greet.

Interviews have typical endings: You and your interviewer part ways, and say goodbye.

Between the beginning and ending you and the interviewer engage in two-way communication.

A job interview is a conversation.

Keep your comments on track, and remain focused on landing the job. You don't want to dominate the discussion, but do offer what you can to help make the conversation interesting, elevating the possibility that you'll land the job.

Go into the Interview with Strength

In the theatre, there's a saying: *Go big, or go home.* Confidence comes from positive self-messages, both those that are conscious and those that are below the level of our conscious thought. Messages from others, both positive and critical ones, can impact our confidence, but only when we choose to believe other peoples' positive or negative reviews of us.

We're especially vulnerable to negative self-talk and more likely to believe critical messages from others when we're tired, anxious, hungry, afraid, stressed, lonely, or ill.

140

The energy you carry with you – the part of you that can't be seen, but is felt – responds to your self-talk, moment-to-moment. Thus, *your* thoughts about yourself affect your resilience and self-worth.

It's your responsibility to ensure that you feel good about yourself, maintain your energy and focus throughout the interview process, and participate in job interviews from a position of strength.

There's no wasted energy.

Every bit of effort you put into preparing for the interview will be obvious to your interviewer. Likewise, if your preparation is inadequate, that will show, too.

Getting the Most from the Interview

As you engage with the interviewer, make the effort to transform any *yes* or *no* answers into full statements that capture what's unique and interesting about you.

You'll have comprehensive and open-ended answers, since you've practiced and rehearsed responses to the variety of typical interview questions in *Chapter 5 – Your Foundation!*

All of your efforts to practice and rehearse will help you fortify your self-confidence. The more you practice, the better.

> # When you have a confident view of yourself, others have confidence in you, too.

As a bottom line, self-confidence tempered with humility is an asset in any job interview. In fact, *assured confidence is a key element in interview success*, as it is in every aspect of a successful life!

Think about you and the person interviewing you as members of the same team. Your responsibilities within the interview process include being prepared, open, and available, while helping make the interviewer's job as easy and pleasant for them as you're able.

The Qualities and Traits the Interviewer Wants You to Reveal

In addition to technical skills and experience, the qualities many interviewers look for are a candidate's personal values, their willingness, and the concern they have for others. These are qualities that you'll *show* them through your actions in the interview.

It's likely your interviewer started gathering information about you from the moment they met you. They're keen to determine if you'll do a good job, whether you'll be a positive influence with customers and co-workers, if you're someone who will be responsive to the company's needs, and if you've got what it takes to continue to grow within the company.

> Your job is to *show* the interviewer their search is over, because in *you* they've found the employee they've been looking for!

The First Thirty Seconds of Your Interview

The first thirty seconds you spend with the interviewer is critical.

The judgments they form about you in those first moments will have an enormous bearing on their decision about whether or not you're a suitable fit for their organization.

> They'll assume what you show them is the best you can offer.

They'll notice the subtle cues and the non-verbal messages you broadcast – how you greet them – whether or not you engage with confidence. They'll notice your handshake, eye contact, and posture. Your comfort or discomfort will be obvious, and so will any awkwardness.

All of this, and much more, is relayed in mere seconds, even before a word is spoken.

As you'll remember, the information recorded in the mind of the interviewer in those first moments is almost impossible to erase, so your job is to present yourself in the best light possible, right out of the gate.

Take a deep breath.

All of the above is true.

> It's also true that employers look for candidates who are confident in their power yet express themselves humbly, and demonstrate integrity, insight, and self-awareness.

You've done your groundwork.

Be yourself. Give your best. Trust the process.

> We relax on the outside when we are settled on the inside.
>
> And vice-versa!

Inside Your Job Interview

After what can seem like an eternity, when the interviewer appears and calls your name, respond with a greeting that feels natural for you, extend your hand, make eye contact, and smile.

Likely the interviewer will introduce him or herself at this point. Confidently acknowledge them with a greeting, such as, *It's nice to meet you*, and refer to them by the name with which they've introduced themselves.

You're interviewing for a job!

As you and the interviewer walk towards the interview room, make a brief comment about your feeling state. You might say something like:

- *I'm excited to be here.*

- *I've been looking forward to this opportunity for a while.*
- *I'm a bit nervous. This is my first interview.*
- *I couldn't wait for today.*
- *I'm feeling a bit overwhelmed but I'm excited at the same time.*

All of these simple statements refer appropriately to what you're experiencing.

Feeling state comments *put you in the room* and give you a chance to immediately break the ice, while they offer a sense of your friendliness, and provide the interviewer with more information about you.

The important message to take from this, is that commenting on how you're feeling is an acceptable way to begin your interview conversation. Your comment allows you to *act* rather than *react* in the situation.

It's also appropriate to tell the interviewer that you're excited and proud to be interviewed for a job with a company that is:

Pick one or two adjectives that honestly reflect your view, or substitute with your own words that reflect something unique and significant about the company.

- Established
- Well-known
- Important
- Respected
- Iconic
- Creative
- Environmentally friendly

146

- Trusted
- Popular
- Historic
- Young and progressive
- Dedicated to health and well-being

Your objective is to be alert and fully present in the interview so you're able to follow wherever the interviewer's questions take you.

Anyone can stumble under the stress of a job interview.

If you suddenly become anxious, and your cognition starts to shut down *(you remember this from Chapter 3)*, and you begin to freeze – don't try to bluff your way through. The interviewer will notice signs of your anxiety even if you think it isn't obvious.

Tell them what's going on!

Here are some examples:

- *It just hit me how nervous I am!*

- *I prepared for the interview, but I guess I didn't realize what it would actually be like to be interviewed.*

- *I'm sorry I missed what you just said. I'm kind of anxious.*

Any of the above statements, or your own words to describe what you're feeling will let the interviewer know that although you're anxious, you're self-aware, and you're committed to keep going with the interview.

You don't have to be the most experienced person being interviewed for the job.

But it helps when you're the most *authentic,* the most *prepared*, and the most *present.*

Everyone is vulnerable at some point in time. One of the biggest mistakes you can make is to pretend to be more in control in a situation than you are.

Your interviewer is most likely to express empathy for you, and they might even tell you about a time their own anxiety surfaced when they were in an important meeting or job interview.

No matter how the interviewer responds to your admission that you feel nervous, you'll notice that when you reveal your anxiety to them, you actually get into the moment, and soothe yourself. This is a beginning stage of recovery.

When you take the risk to talk with the interviewer about your nervous reaction, you should soon be able to gather your thoughts again. Make eye contact, and relax your jaw. You might be able to smile. In any event, you'll have enough recovery to go forward with the interview.

If *at any time* a person's questions or behavior deeply trigger your anxiety, and/or you feel uncomfortable with questions that demand too much information, or comments that are inappropriately suggestive – *this can happen, even in a job interview* – it's your right to say, *I don't know how to answer your question, but thank you for your interest and your time. I'm going to leave now.* Don't hesitate. Get on your feet and leave.

Your feelings are valid. There's no reason to remain in a situation in which you feel – at *any* level – that you're at risk. Politely excuse yourself from the conversation, and leave immediately.

> There's no need to apologize for what you decide to tell someone, or how much, or how little you tell them.

And you're entitled to leave a situation when *you* decide it's time.

It's your choice. Having healthy boundaries is an important starting point to any conversation or relationship.

As always, you're in charge.

Decide first whether or not you feel *comfortable,* and whether or not you *trust* the person. If the answers are *yes,* then go for it, and give it your best in the interview.

Keep in mind that interviews are meant to be *two-way conversations.*

Interviews are a chance for you to find out about the job and the company so you can decide if the job is a fit for you.

And interviews are an opportunity for the interviewer to learn about you.

The interviewer has a need they want to fill. They've invested time and effort into meeting you. Thus, you've become a significant part of their process, as they search for the best person to do the job for which they're hiring. How you respond to their questions will determine how, at this advanced stage in the hiring process, they assess your value to the company.

I can assure you, *the interviewer wants their search to be over*, and *they'll be thrilled if you're the employee they've been looking for!*

> While you're in the interview, envision your interaction with the interviewer as the start of a new relationship.

Take your time when you respond to their questions.

Keep your replies confident and thoughtful, and present yourself as a worthy and capable person.

> Answer honestly, and offer some personal insight, which will build the interviewer's trust in you and your abilities.

You'll create rapport with the interviewer by being your authentic self.

Use your time in the interview to ask questions so you can learn about the job for which you're applying, as well as get a feel for the company, business, or organization. This information will help you decide if the company is a good fit for you.

Job interviews by nature can provoke fear, even if you're familiar with the organization or business.

Learning to recover from anxious feelings and distress is a great reason to practice answering interview questions with an ally. Any amount of interpersonal practice is enormously useful.

No matter how many interviews you may have experienced in the past, it can be terrifying to open yourself to questioning, and provide information to someone you've just met. No matter what, maintain soft eye contact.

> *Soft eye contact is a learned skill that allows you to remain focused on the other person while comfortably shifting your gaze away momentarily, and then returning to eye contact with them.*

If you're distressed, and you want to break soft eye contact with the interviewer, and you're aware that you're beginning to shut down, do whatever you can *not* to break eye contact.

In distress, we tend to pull back, or even break connection with the other person. I encourage you to take the opportunity to practice recovery during minor conflicts with family members and friends, before you're in an actual interview situation.

After shutting down or retreating it's challenging to recover and return to eye contact. To avoid this discomfort, when you're momentarily anxious, see if you're able to resist the urge to pull back, and do whatever you can to maintain eye contact. *Take a risk and talk about your nervousness instead!*

The exception is any unsafe situation, as discussed earlier. If someone's questions, comments, or behaviour activate your anxiety, and you're uncomfortable about the personal nature and scope of the questions – even if you're in an interview for a job– you're entitled to set a limit. It's your right to say:

> *I don't know how to answer your question,*
> *but thank you for your interest and your*
> *time. I'm going to leave now.*

Don't hesitate. Get on your feet and leave.

On the other hand, in an interview situation in which you feel safe, despite your nervousness, do what you can to maintain soft eye contact while you interact.

Above all, do your best to stay present in the face of your discomfort.

Even when an interview is challenging, do your best to push through and keep going.

Focus, on the interviewer's eyes, or at least on their face!

Be truthful and let the interviewer know:

Interviews are new for me.

I got off-track and felt anxious for a moment.

I think I'm okay now.

Memorize and practice saying these sentences until you're able to recite them when you wake in the middle of the night.

You never know if and when you'll need to re-set during an interview.

These sentences are a life-line to have onboard that you can toss to yourself.

Moreover, the sentiment contained in these life-line statements can come in handy at *any time* and in *any situation* in which you find yourself struggling with anxious feelings.

Call on your willpower, maintain eye contact, swap out the word *interviews* from the statement, and substitute the situation in which you presently find yourself.

When you use the statements and trust the process, they'll lead you to freedom.

After you've made your way back from a nervous or anxious state, the experience itself affirms your resilience.

The process of recovery from a bout of anxiety can be extraordinary to witness. Your interviewer will have every reason to be impressed!

At any point in an interview you can become overwhelmed.

But even when you're nervous there's always something for you to give back – you might provide a brief example to illustrate an answer, or reflect a question back to the interviewer, which can help gain their rapport, simply by asking, *Do you know what I mean?*

When you're being interviewed for a job, it's important to be open and transparent. You might think that when someone asks you to tell them about yourself, they'll want to know *everything*. They don't.

And even if they did, you're not required in any interview, or in any social situation to disclose private details about yourself. No one expects that of you. They don't want to hear it. You don't want to tell it. Too much information is too much information.

Each of us gets to decide *to whom* to tell something, *what* to tell them, *how much* to tell, and *if and when* it's an appropriate time to tell.

Exit the Interview with Strength

As you say goodbye, don't wait for the interviewer to extend their hand to you to signal the end of the meeting. Reach your hand forward in a friendly, firm handshake.

Tell them you enjoyed meeting them, and that you appreciate the time they spent with you. Thank them and say their name.

Wrap up with, *I look forward to hearing back from you. When do you think you'll make your decision?*

If they say they should know within several days, or in a week, you can respond accordingly. *If I haven't heard from you, is it okay if I call you in (several days) a week?* or *I'll call in several days to follow up. How should I remind you about me and my interview?*

When you exit a job interview from a position of strength and confidence you leave behind a powerful parting message, along with a clear opportunity for you to reconnect in a short period of time.

> ## No matter what happens, you own this experience.

No one can take your experience away from you. If you land the job, kudos! If you don't land the job, kudos! There's no wasted energy. You've had an experience, you've put forth your best. Each time it gets easier.

> ## Every step you take outside your comfort zone reflects your inner journey. You've come so far!

After Your Job Interview

Never underestimate the massive number of applicants for entry-level and service positions! You're one of many.

Let your courtesy and preparation set you apart from all of the other candidates who are competing for the same job.

To make an impression and stand apart from other applicants, immediately after the interview write a thank-you email, which is a great opportunity to respond in a simple, reliable format following your interview. Remind the interviewer that you'll be in touch shortly to follow up.

On the email subject line, type *Thank you*. Your message should be short, enthusiastic, and to the point, as illustrated below:

Dear _____,

Thank you for taking the time to meet with me this morning (afternoon) to discuss the _____ position with the XYZ Company.

After hearing more about the position, I am excited about this opportunity and I'm confident that my (*communication, previous, etc.*) skills and extensive (*volunteer, hands-on, etc.*) experience at _____ make me a perfect fit for the job!

As we discussed at the end of my interview, I will be in touch with you by phone (*email*) on _____ to follow up on your decision.

Please feel free to contact me in the meantime if you have any questions.

Regards,

Ensure that you <u>follow up with the interviewer</u> to enquire if a decision has been made, in the agreed-upon time frame you discussed at the conclusion of your interview, by telephone (or in an email if they've specified that mode of communication).

The tone of your phone call or email should be upbeat and confident.

> Sometimes a nudge by phone or
> email is enough for an employer
> to decide to offer the job to you,
> the eager applicant who's online,
> or perhaps, on the line.

Although thank you emails are widely accepted, the exception might occur with career professionals or candidates for high-level management positions, where, immediately following the interview they might compose and hand-deliver, or send a formal thank-you letter by regular mail.

It's Time to Celebrate When

- Your phone rings and you hear the person on the line say, *Congratulations, you've been selected to fill the position!*

- You open your email messages and find a message from the person who interviewed you, inviting you to an orientation for the job for which you've just found out you've been hired.

- You're hired on the spot at your interview.

When any of these things happen, it's time to celebrate! Out of countless applicants who competed for the position, you're the one who landed the job! Let that sink in.

> ## You've practiced and rehearsed for what seems like forever, and that's what it takes.

All those hours you searched, examined your thoughts, and dug deep.

All of the insights you wrote about in your notebook.

All of the times you talked yourself off a ledge and recommitted yourself to engaging fully in this process.

All of the tears you may have shed.

All of the anxieties and fears you soothed.

All of the setbacks you faced and the losses you endured.

All of the pain and the growing edges you explored.

All of the times your inner strengths rallied, surfaced, and fought their way into the light.

> You've earned trust in your abilities, and belief in yourself.
>
> All of it was worth it!
>
> Congratulations!

If You Didn't Make It This Time

Sometimes life doesn't go the way we planned. There's always a chance we'll fail to reach our intended goal.

Having to grieve a lost opportunity is a possibility whenever we risk and step outside our comfort zone. The journey isn't always easy, and even though we might want something with every bit of who we are, sometimes there are just too many hoops to jump through.

> Disappointment stings. It hurts.

> As with any loss in life, you must allow yourself to feel your sadness, and then move on.

Life is a series of steps forward and back through tears and joy, each step back encouraging you to correct your course, and advance again.

The pain and frustration at not landing the job can be a useful nudge for you to acknowledge your strengths, in spite of the loss.

You're in rich territory, filled with lessons and growth that wouldn't have emerged if you hadn't risked.

You've worked hard, and you've made a tremendous effort. In the moment, it can be difficult to see that there could be any benefit in not realizing the dream of landing the job you'd set your heart on.

If you view the setback as an indication that you're not worthy enough to succeed, reject this belief. It does not affirm the strengths you've claimed, nor the valuable human that is you.

Sometimes we step out beyond our comfort zone, just a bit too far. Setbacks give us respite, and they provide a temporary pause, time to catch our breath and recalibrate.

As you affirm your intention to continue on your journey of growth, use your setbacks as opportunities to shine some light on places within yourself that may have been overlooked when you explored your strengths and your developing needs, during your interview preparation.

Setbacks contain at least one lesson as well as an opportunity to reaffirm your desire. And setbacks act as a signal to re-set your intention for success.

Make a radical shift and allow yourself to reframe any judgment of failure.

You might ask your wise self, *what could I do in the future to strengthen myself in this area?* Listen and follow your inner sage, and despite your disappointment in the moment, you'll have planted the seeds for your future success.

It's important to remember that everything in your job search, aside from your own experience, is out of your hands, and will always be decided by someone else.

> You've done your work, and you're ready to hear this: *you're resilient. You can take whatever comes.*

As you go forward, the more you allow yourself to face your losses, one safe step at a time, with mindfulness – the closer you'll be to achieving what you want.

> When you're ready, you know what to do.

Pull out your notebook, write out your intention, and start preparing for your next job interview!

One day soon you'll celebrate, too.

> You've got this!

A Note for Job Search Coaches

Job Interview – Anxious? You've Got This! is effective one-to-one as a coaching model. The model can also be facilitated to guide senior high school students and college grads towards employment, within a 13-week semester format in the classroom, or as an adjunct program in weekly meetings reinforced by support pairs, led by a volunteer parent, teacher, or student peer.

The model is also effective as a Continuing Studies program, offered for new arrivals who may require assistance to prepare for interviews; and for adults who are fearful, or uncertain of the steps required to enter or re-enter the workforce.

The *Job Interview* model might also be offered to youth and adult participants who struggle with anxiety disorders, in a series of supported weekly sessions facilitated within the community by Community Mental Health Workers, Social Workers, Mental Health counsellors, and Employment and Assistance Workers.

For more information and to arrange volume purchase discounts of *Job Interview – Anxious? You've Got This!* or to enquire about presentations, workshops, and private coaching, email val@youthinterview.com or visit www.youthinterview.com

Essential Supplies for Your Job-Seeking Journey

One or more lined notebooks

> An essential need. Consider them to be as important as would be a map or compass when you embark on a journey.

Small notebook or journal for your bedside

> Useful for recording thoughts that enter your mind just before sleep, your agenda for the following day, nighttime affirmations, a sleep log of your bedtime and waking times, and anything else that comes to mind before bed or upon waking.

Post-it notes or coloured binder tabs

> Essential for tagging important passages in *Job Interview – Anxious? You've Got This!* and marking and distinguishing written notations in your lined notebook, and organizing book and notebook sections, all of which will make it easier for you to focus on your process. If you don't want to purchase Post-it notes or binder tabs, you might cut out tab-size bits from colourful magazine advertisements and attach to your pages with clear tape or paper glue.

Coloured highlighters

> Vital tools for highlighting significant passages in your book and notebook. As with Post-it notes and binder tabs, I suggest you use a rainbow range of colours, in both the highlighters you choose for your text, and gel pens or fine markers for your written work, which will help stimulate your creative brain and boost your mood. As stated, these are vital tools. Think: colour = enhanced creativity = temporary freedom from worrying thoughts. Start out with whatever highlighters and pens you can afford.

Magazine clippings of words, phrases, and pictures with which you resonate

> Creativity and confidence enhancers. Gathering and collecting colourful printed symbols, words, and phrases for your notebook is a soothing activity in which I encourage you to engage frequently. Powers-up your imagination, in much the same way as a collage or wish-box. Your brain will thank you for every effort you make to spend moments in your inventive mind, since anxiety cannot find any space in there!

Activity Checklist

Preface pages xi - xx

Flip-side behaviour
start doing one thing differently from the way in which you would typically do it

Change your thinking
prompt your mind
think it, see it, say it, do it

Be intentional choose behaviours that will become habits that support you

Add new habits
expand your present routine around nutrition, sleep, movement, exercise

Stay present incorporate a mini practice of meditation and mindfulness

Journal and record
write down your thoughts

Explore creativity
activate your imagination

Chapter 1 – Your Journey   pages 3 - 17

Compassion
be kind to yourself

engage an ally

Chapter 2 – Your Tools   pages 21 - 45

Imagination
use it intentionally and sensibly
imagine doing or saying something you fear
challenge yourself to practice, despite your fear

Attention
the skill of focusing your thinking on what's happening in the moment

Intention
your statement should be specific and concrete
state your intention as if it is already actualized, in the present tense
make it measurable – how much, when, and where
predict the feeling tone your intention will bring, as if it has already happened
read aloud several times daily

Choice (Risk and Trust)
engage fully in some approximation of risk, even for a very short time
try a new behavior on for one minute at a time
extend your risk readiness by one minute more at a time, and so on

Mirror exercise
stand in front of a well-lit mirror and gaze into your own eyes

Sleep regulation
record your bedtimes and waking times
journal your thoughts about sleep regulation

Strength Contract
'I AM' statement
record your strength contract in your notebook
repeat your strength contract aloud over and over,
daily

Talk to the Eyes
look into the eyes of the people around you and *talk
to the eyes*.
think to yourself, *I'm looking at brown eyes,* or
whatever eyes you see

Life Altering Words and Phrases
jot in your notebook, practice and read aloud
frequently
fit the words and phrases into daily conversations with
others

Can you tell me about yourself?
prepare and memorize a casual reply
prepare and memorize a professional response geared
towards the job you want

Self-Acknowledge
list the concrete results you have already achieved in
your life, or
list the qualities that make you a good human
(empathy, respect for others)

Positive Self-Statements
from this point forward, think and speak about
yourself with respect

Chapter 3 – Your Fears   pages 49 - 61

The Fear Response

The Anxiety Response

Fear, Anxiety and the Brain: A Mindful Approach

Nerd Declaration
lovingly repeat the ultimate affirmation,
with a smile, every day

Chapter 4 – Your Focus   pages 65 - 79

Who You Are

Strengths and Personal Attributes
give examples of how and when you demonstrated
each quality

Accomplishments and Achievements
in your notebook list several

Skills

Interests   choose 2 or 3 to discuss in your interview

Future Hopes and Dreams
use action words and jot in your notebook

Chapter 5 – Your Foundation   pages 83 - 116

References   list 2 or more in your notebook
obtain phone numbers and email addresses
give your references a heads-up

Certificates   photocopy awards and diplomas and place in large
envelope

Your Resume search online for functional resume template (for
entry level job)
search for a chronological resume template if you
have a work history
keep to one page
brief narrative of your strengths, skills, and attributes
use answers you harvested from Chapter 4 - The Focus
to guide you

Application form template

prepare in advance
copy your references and contact information onto
the form
fill in all spaces

Core Job Interview Question: Can you tell me about yourself?

review Chapter 2
review Chapter 4, prepare a first draft in your
notebook
practice your script daily

Typical Interview Questions

take time and think about your answers. Be authentic
write out each question. Record each answer
have a concrete example for each answer written down
use full, personalized sentences
practice frequently

Your questions for the Interviewer

prepare at least 2 *what* and *how* questions specific to the company

Chapter 6 – The Job Interview Process

pages 119 - 131

Job Seeking Tasks

Clothing   research to establish company dress code and norms
keep your clothing choices simple
gather and prepare your interview attire well in advance

The Information Interview

research the best person with whom to meet
call to obtain their email address
email requesting a 15-minute meeting to gather information
prepare questions
following the interview, compose and send a thank-you email

Chapter 7 – The Job Interview – Your Best Foot Forward

Leading up to the Job Interview
Re-read Chapter 6 – The Job Interview Process and study the entire chapter

When your anxiety is deeply triggered or you feel uncomfortable with a person
practice saying *I don't know how to answer your question, but thank you for your interest and your time. I'll be leaving now.*

Your lifeline – when you want to recover and keep going
Practice saying *Interviews are new for me. I got off-track and felt anxious for a moment. I think I'm okay now.*

After the job interview
immediately send a thank-you email
follow-up with your interviewer by telephone or email, as agreed

If You Didn't Make It This Time

About the Author

Val's enthusiasm as an advocate for unemployed and under-employed individuals spans decades. She has over thirty years' experience as a lecturer and consultant in Organization Development during which she facilitated Management and Supervisory training, and instructed college and university classes in Interpersonal Communication.

In the late 80's, having observed first-hand the barriers to employment that are faced by youth, Val co-founded a private trade school, now an accredited college, aimed at supporting unemployed youth and youth at risk to gain labour market skills. Val introduced a practicum model along with co-op employment strategies. She developed life skills modules, trades math upgrading and pre-apprenticeship curricula for youth, trades equivalency training and worksite placements for new arrivals to Canada, accredited ECCE training, and hands-on technical training for women in non-traditional employment in the construction, electrical, and plumbing trades. She also piloted several long-running job search programs funded by both federal and provincial governments.

In addition to writing about workplace issues, Val provides vocational support to adolescents and young adults. You can follow Val's work at www.youthinterview.com

Dr. Roy Holland and Val Hunter are co-authors of *Parenting: The Joy and Pain – An Exploration of Mindful Attachment Parenting*, available for purchase on Amazon in eBook and print.

Made in the USA
San Bernardino,
CA

58386005R00127